THE HIGH-FLYING
ADVENTURES
OF CAPTAIN GRIEF

THE HIGH-FLYING ADVENTURES OF CAPTAIN GRIEF

A MEMOIR ABOUT LAUGHING IN THE FACE OF DEATH

Dear Katie & Rupert
Thank you for being so aware and open and giving you are the best. Much love
Kelly

KELLY WILK

ILLUSTRATIONS BY CHARLES HACKBARTH

IGUANA

Copyright © 2024 Kelly Wilk
Published by Iguana Books
720 Bathurst Street
Toronto, ON M5S 2R4

All rights reserved. No part of this publication may be reproduced, stored in a retrieval system or transmitted, in any form or by any means, electronic, mechanical, recording or otherwise (except brief passages for purposes of review) without the prior permission of the author.

Okay ... so, peeps, a note about Kelly's brain. It's foggy at best, even without the grief brain. Suffice to say, Kelly's recollections of the events of 2013 and beyond are written as she remembers them, the dialogue has been re-created to the best of her ability, so give her some slack, she was a mess! The only possibly offensive stuff in this memoir should be from me. You're welcome.
— Captain Grief

Publisher: Cheryl Hawley
Editor: Paula Chiarcos
Illustrations: Charles Hackbarth

ISBN 978-1-77180-695-4 (paperback)
ISBN 978-1-77180-696-1 (hardcover)
ISBN 978-1-77180-697-8 (epub)

This is an original print edition of *The High-Flying Adventures of Captain Grief*.

Thank you to all my friends and family who have loved and supported me and helped me get through what has been one of the hardest times of my life.

Thank you to all the people I love who will always be with me in spirit, to heckle, to encourage, and to laugh along with me.

And thank you to my hero, Captain Grief. Go back to the Alps for a well-earned vacation! Hang out with that goat herder you convinced to be your wedding-cake topper. See if he will come party and provide the beer!

FOREWORD

As a clinical psychologist, I have had years of training and experience with helping clients navigate grief. Sadness and loss are realities of the human experience. I find that they are frequently present in psychotherapy sessions, even if they are not the original reason a person reaches out for therapy.

I met Kelly early on in my educational pursuits to become a psychologist when we both attended the University of Guelph for our undergraduate degrees. Kelly and I have been friends now for over 20 years and I also considered her partner, Kara, to be a close friend. I remember when Kelly met Kara, it became clear that their relationship was truly one that many hope to experience: a relationship filled with love, caring, humour and deep connection. Kelly and Kara's wedding was a memorable celebration overflowing with the love and support of family and friends. A few of us snuck into the wedding suite at the hotel while Kelly and Kara were distracted with the festivities. We left well wishes and treats for them to find and enjoy later. It was truly a celebratory atmosphere. Kara was a solid friend whom you could count on for anything from a bear hug to a good laugh to survivalist advice. She once itemized for me the supplies she on hand should there be a sudden emergency evacuation of the city.

When Kara died suddenly after a relatively brief period of illness in 2012, it was hard to accept that such a loss could happen. I witnessed Kelly's journey with grief, and continue to experience it myself. When Kelly asked me to write the foreword for *Captain Grief*, I was honoured. I also found the process daunting as despite all of my training and knowledge surrounding grief, it was difficult to face and sit with my own sadness. The emotional pain and the emptiness that followed after Kara's death was hard for everyone who had been fortunate enough to know her. The emotional pain that Kelly has carried since that day is tenfold. Not only did Kelly lose her spouse, but she also suddenly found herself in the role of single parent to their one-year-old son. She lost the future she and Kara had dreamed about. Her entire world was shaken up, never to be the same. Grieving is hard. Grieving the death of a spouse unexpectedly at a young age is harder still. Navigating that grief in a world that does not fully support same-sex couples adds yet another layer of difficulty.

The sudden death of a spouse at a young age is described in bereavement literature as profound and life-altering. While spousal loss at an older age has been well researched, the experiences of young widows and widowers, particularly those in the 2SLGBTQ+ community, are just beginning to be heard. Young surviving spouses experience both a loss of companionship and the loss of a shared future consisting of hopes and dreams. There is often a significant financial impact as well. Those with children find themselves adjusting to parenting alone at the same time that they are living through the "firsts" without their life partner. Same-sex marriage was legalized only 20 years ago in Canada and has still yet to be recognized in many places in the world. Surviving spouses in the 2SLGBTQ+ community are grieving in the context of a society that may not recognize, rally around, or provide support in the same way that it may be readily offered for a person grieving the death of a heterosexual spouse. When grief is unacknowledged or invalidated, the grief becomes hidden, which creates difficulty navigating through the grieving process, commonly known as disenfranchised grief. A person experiencing disenfranchised grief may feel overwhelmingly alone and unsupported.

Out of Kelly's grief grew a desire to process what she was feeling and use her writing and creativity as an outlet. She created Captain Grief, the hero she needed to find the strength to carry on. After reading her early blog posts I found myself wiping away tears and at the same time laughing at the antics of Captain Grief. It takes real bravery to face sorrow and write about personal experiences in navigating this significant loss, let alone share these experiences publicly. Over time, Kelly's blog posts grew in number and she started hearing from others who were navigating their own losses. Kelly has captured a young widow's experience in this queer memoir in a way that is accessible and relatable to others. Kelly's reflections are raw, honest, sad, brutal, dark, funny and playful. She captures the messiness of continuing to live in the face of profound loss. Captain Grief will no doubt be a story that others who have lost a partner can see themselves in, and find comfort in not being alone in their experiences. While Kelly initially made a decision to help process her grief through her writing, she ultimately created a piece of work that can now serve as a guidepost to others navigating their personal journeys of devastating grief and loss.

Amberley Buxton, Ph.D., C.Psych.
Clinical Psychologist

PROLOGUE
YOU DYING WAS *NOT* THE PLAN

I was never a comic-book kid. But on Saturday mornings you could find this lipstick lesbian in the making watching *Jem and the Holograms*, *She-Ra: Princess of Power*, or *Batman*, where I patiently awaited the sultry arrival of Catwoman — though no power femme could hold a candle to Lynda Carter's Wonder Woman. Season One, "Bullets and Bracelets," first aired in 1975 and was seared into my cortex. I still have flashbacks of the Amazonian goddess spinning herself into her magical costume, brandishing accessories that doubled as weapons.

While I was busy running around the house and jumping off stools in my Wonder Woman underwear, I was also trying on something else — power — and not just the best way to brush off a bullet or throw my tiara at someone.

Wonder Woman demonstrated the Divine Feminine, with strength, self-sufficiency, confidence, and perseverance. The idea of *power* has spun its way into my imagination since I was little — but little girls grow up. In the world of holistic healing, I have witnessed many women, including myself, lose that spark. I've seen how they find it so difficult to stand in their power, understanding that it is, in fact, who they truly are.

Of all the things Wonder Woman taught me, the most important is that choice is power. As long as you can make a decision for yourself, you can find your happiness. I've relied on this lesson throughout my life. Even so, I never had much opportunity to lean into it — until the fall of 2012 when, at the age of thirty-four, I suddenly became a widow.

My world was thrown into chaos. I'd lost a parent at the age of nineteen, so I knew grief. But this left me alone, a single mother of a nineteen-month-old son, new and frightening territory. As a writer, I knew I would journal to move through the grieving process, but I didn't anticipate the accompanying laughter.

After Kara died, several things helped me. My mother made to-do lists, organized paperwork, and did the laundry. My friends supported me through the funeral arrangements, brought me groceries, made phone calls, and babysat. My belly-dancing teacher offered me free classes, and my writing coach, Chris Kay Fraser, delivered home-cooked meals. I was uplifted by the massive show of love — although the most unexpected support came from *me*.

When Chris offered me a space in her blogging workshop, I worried it might not fit the therapeutic writing projects I had in mind. I had a fledgling poetry blog, so I thought my urgency to express myself might motivate me. At first I was overwhelmed by the information she gave us, but in the onslaught of useful ideas there was one tantalizing tip that dangled in front of my eyes long enough to hook me — to create a fictional character to blog with (who ended up starring in this very book you are reading).

Memories stirred. Hadn't I spent hours in the library in high school geeking out, writing spoofs to share with a cartoonist pal? Hadn't I created a fictional character to embody my struggles with chronic pain? (More on that later.) I can see her in my mind, teeth glinting, purple cape flying, hands anchored on hips in the quintessential superhero pose. It then occurred to me: I don't need a poetry blog, I need a superhero!

That day at the workshop I wrote a list: *Twelve things that would normally be frowned upon or misunderstood, but that you can get away with when your spouse dies.* Then I laughed — out loud. Something I hadn't done since my wife died. Then the other people in the workshop laughed, and friends and family on social media laughed, in an exuberant, emotional, relieved manner. I was invigorated. I'd made people laugh. I'd given myself permission to be as bitter or saucy or tortured or dramatic or messy or bitchy or funny as I wanted to be. I felt free!

It's not a surprise that, when I wanted to put a face to my caped crusader, I thought of my cartoonist friend, Stephanie Fahey, who was doing graphic design and animation for children's shows. The first sketch she sent me was perfect: tall boots, long cape, stereotypically small mask that would fool only innocent bystanders in a comic-book world.

It was wonderful, except for the facial expression. It looked like my superhero was a little down after riding the bus all the way to the library and then realizing she'd forgotten her library card.

"I need more," I told her. "I need her to be screaming or bawling her face off."

The moment Stephanie came back and told me how she had giggled as she drew the new wailing face, my alter ego, Captain Grief, was born. And she was just what I needed. Grief is messy ... and I needed a space to be all the things I felt, without human limitations. Captain Grief is a superhero and I wanted to feel super too.

The Captain and I took flight together on February 14, 2013. I was entering the Year of Firsts, and the first hurdle was Valentine's Day. It fell on a Thursday, so I figured, why not? Every Thursday for a year, the Captain and I would get together and write. On that first day, we wrote a piece called "Valentine's Day Sucks" and something happened while writing: We found it also *didn't* suck in major ways. Sure, I grieved the tidal wave of a widow on Valentine's Day, but I also focused on my writing — and had fun doing it.

Sometimes I thought I couldn't bear to turn the horror of particular weeks into hilarity. Many Wednesday nights, I had nothing but a blank screen and a sweaty brow. Despite that, I made my fingers move and wrote until I found "it": that one thing that happened during the week that made it possible to move from painful to playful.

I didn't think I could maintain it, but after a while I trusted that something would present itself to laugh at. Humour slowly transformed my life. I started to feel a little joy. There was still a deep crevasse of bereavement running through my life, but now I had the superpowers to cross it — to counter the social awkwardness and the pain, loneliness, and isolation that grief drops on your doorstep.

I also think this is the way my wife would have wanted me to deal with her death. She was always the first person to remind me that I had the choice to laugh. Captain Grief also gave me a vehicle to provide reassurance, catharsis, and healing for family and friends who missed Kara and who were terribly concerned about how my son, Ben (aka, The Ginger Menace), and I were doing. With Captain Grief, I battled sugary supervillains, rip-your-guts-out anniversaries, smarmy mall music, ginger temper tantrums, and my penchant for accidentally lighting things on fire. More on that later.

We also talked about my dad, to honour his memory and keep him close. With Captain Grief at my side, it felt so good to talk about my wife every week, to share funny stories, like the time I cleaned out her car and found an axe and a twenty-year-old bottle of port.

Through my writing, I encountered other queer widows who asked me how I knew so much about their lives. My need to express myself, coupled with my impulse to be visible and unapologetic, set Captain Grief and me on a new course for life. In the process, we've provided the space for other people to do what we're doing: thriving in spite of our grief. I feel grateful, proud, expansive, successful, and powerful.

Writing as — and with — a grieving, queer superhero taught me a lot about grief. I talked about going in and out of the seven stages ad nauseam, but as a few months turned into six, and then twelve, I noticed a shift. Captain Grief was showing up less often, and when she did, she would mercilessly call me out for my neglect. I guess you could say it was an exercise in self-punishment, or a really cool way to have an argument with myself. Although she had a point. And with true unapologetic, mildly brutal Captain Grief flare, she wrote me a greeting card: "You created a superhero alter ego, and you're using her as a crutch. Just give it up and go eat some cake!"

She wasn't always so thoughtful, but she was right.

I recently told a friend and fellow writer how guilty I felt about leaving Captain Grief behind. Even though it made me want to vomit to admit it, I worried whether I could do it without her. Would readers still find me funny or interesting if I wrote solely as me?

"Kelly..." My friend took a moment so this would sink in. "You *are* Captain Grief." Talk about putting on the power.

For much of that Year of Firsts, friends and family encouraged me to "Put on the cape!" And I would bravely deck myself out in my fabulous glamour gear and charge ahead. She was my running start, my placeholder for the "me" that one day I would remember I was. I didn't have to put on a cape — I was born with it! A slinky yellow cape, bitchin' boots, and one hell of an attitude.

Either way, whether it's Captain Grief writing or me, there will always be laughter, gratitude, remembrance, celebration, and tears. There will be toasts with port, and to my wife, who is chortling away from heaven, I say, "Ha! This laugh is on me."

** WARNING **

This book is filled with intense emotional highs and lows, catfights, potty mouths, death, destruction, turmoil, and bad puns.

Do not undertake the reading of this lightly!

Extreme super-serious list of items to prepare for reading this book:

1. A change of clothing. Grief is messy.
2. Copious amounts of tissue.
3. Drops for dry eye.
4. Ten-mile radius from impressionable children, especially ones that lip-read.
5. Or a swear jar.
6. Bandages in case of paper cuts (or lemons if you need a good cry).
7. Gel-pack eye mask to come back from the good cry.
8. Cape.
9. Flying licence optional, but highly recommended.
10. Medication for motion sickness of all kinds.
11. Cake.

Also, anyone opposed to time travel, please put this book down.

*A version of this prologue was originally published in *PinkPlayMags* springplay! issue, 2015.

CONTENTS

FOREWORD	V
PROLOGUE	IX
WARNING	XV
CHAPTER ONE: CAPTAIN GRIEF TAKES FLIGHT	**1**
Valentine's Day Sucks	2
Patrick Swayze Needs A Talking To	4
When Grief Is Awkward	5
Retreat, Retreat!	7
Channelling Judith Viorst	10
Captain Grief And The Terrible, Horrible, No Good, Very Bad Day	11
Where She Isn't…	14
CHAPTER TWO: I CAN CRY IF I WANT TO … DAMN IT	**17**
When Aliens Weep	21
Regrets About Granola	24
Grief Brain Dog-Sits	27
My Nemesis Is Lemon	31
CHAPTER THREE: THERE'S NOTHING WRONG WITH CAKE	**37**
The Queer Widows/Widowers Convention	40
1. Comatose Coffee House (Shock And Denial)	41
2. The Guilt Gauntlet (Pain And Guilt)	41
3. The Bargaining Bazaar (Anger And Bargaining)	42
4. Bleeding Heart Café (Depression And Loneliness)	42
5. Upwards Turn Annex (Upwards Turn)	42
6. Reconstruction Zone (Reconstruction)	43
7. Club Acceptance (Acceptance)	43
Capitan Grief Vs. Sweet Tooth	43
CHAPTER FOUR: FEELING SORRY FOR YOURSELF… IS ACTUALLY A STAGE	**51**
Shrines Are Fine	54
Breakneck Learning Curve	55

Toddler Coping Styles	58
She Can Be Taught	61
International Widows Day	65
Post-Pride Slump	68

CHAPTER FIVE: "I GOT THE POWER!" — 73

My Butch Wife	77
Flood Of Grief	80
Under My Skin	84
Captain Pouty-Pants Uninvites Me To A Party	93

CHAPTER SIX: GETTING ON WITH IT ISN'T GETTING OVER IT, BUT YOU HAVE TO START SOMEWHERE — 100

Be Nice To Hamsters	106
Is It Just Me Or Is This Helping?	108
Laughing At Myself	111
Creative Licence	114
Alpine	116

CHAPTER SEVEN: HOLIDAYS CAN KICK YOUR ASS — 119

Super Imposters	123
If It Ain't Broke	130
Waiting For Santa	138
Found Poetry From Personal Ads	140

CHAPTER EIGHT: GRIEF FUCKS UP YOUR LIFE, BUT YOU MAKE IT WORK — 142

Burn	150
Kara Sends Me A Peacock	158
Memos From The Universe	162
Half Baked	166
Funny Valentine	169

EPILOGUE — 180

AUTHOR'S NOTE — 185

Pop Quiz	189
Trivial Pursuit: The Kara Edition	190
Bonus Round	191

ABOUT THE AUTHOR — 193

BIBLIOGRAPHY — 195

CHAPTER ONE
CAPTAIN GRIEF TAKES FLIGHT

And now is the moment you get to meet my alter ego, Captain Grief, my personal caped crusader, unapologetically making her way through the infuriating, embarrassing, impolite stages of grief, and then backtracking quickly.

Is she moody?

She sure is.

Prone to indecisiveness?

Heck, yeah.

Seems a little slower than her usual self?

You betcha.

Bit of a slob?

Sometimes.

Likely to break into uncontrollable fits of sobbing in public?

Without a doubt.

She's kind of a bitch too, but that's allowed. She's grieving after all — in a cape!

VALENTINE'S DAY SUCKS

So there I was all alone waiting for Captain Grief, my partner in crime, to show her masked face. *Happy freaking Valentine's Day!* My toddler had a meltdown as I dropped him off at daycare that morning. I could barely get him out of the stroller to go inside. After that I bought red roses for my own damn self. They made me happy, and I couldn't have them around when my wife was alive, as she was allergic to them. And they went well with the chocolate Turtles I bought and the large brown plush bear holding a cheesy pink heart, which was for my kid, but really for me. So I was all ready to go, when I received an email from Captain Grief, which went something like this:

Hey, Kel. Sorry, dude, I can't make the launch. Did you get my card? I can't get out of bed. My face is crusted to the pillow because of all the crying. I lost my voice from wailing, and I had a horrible dream last night about a giggling cupid poking me over and over again with an arrow, singing, "No Val-en-tine for you; no Val-en-tine for you!" Whose brilliant idea was this anyway? To start a blog paying tribute to our dead wives on national Expensive Candy Day? Do we have to do it today? Anyway, they should be fired. Can you look into that? — CG.

The card she sent me was pretty great. It perked me up enough to help me write my first list.

Nine things to do when Valentine's Day SUCKS because your spouse died...

1. Go to bed. Things will be the same in the morning, but at least Valentine's Day will be over.

2. Make a pillow person, dress them up in your spouse's shirt and pants (hat optional) and spray liberally with their cologne, perfume, or deodorant. Then revisit first suggestion.

3. Sit the pillow person at the table and order in.

4. Purge your feelings by watching romantic movies where one of the spouses dies and then wail copiously into your popcorn.

5. Take a shower, revoke the ban on shaving, and get out of the house. Get some of your single pals together and go dancing. If need be, slow dance with one and cry on their shoulder.

6. Ask your friends to write cards for you. Everybody needs love, especially you, right now!

7. Heart-shaped piñata. Baseball bat à la Jennifer Garner in *Valentine's Day*.

8. Purge your feelings by listening to songs that rip your guts out, all night, on a loop. I highly recommend "All I Want Is You" by U2.

9. Eat icing out of the jar.

PATRICK SWAYZE NEEDS A TALKING TO

"Oh man, you killed me last week," said Captain Grief as we sat down for a chai latté. She was obviously still riddled with post-Valentine's sorrow.

"I watched *Ghost*. Man, Patrick Swayze is a dink!" she said.

"Totally," I answered. (By that, I mean to say, Swayze's character, Sam, in the epic love-after-life story. It is *not* to malign his awesome dirty-dancing self in any way!)

Sam jumps the express train to the afterlife and is caught in limbo. He has a mission to solve his own murder, but also ample time to watch his widow (I hate that word) grieve. His wife, Molly, played by the lovely Demi Moore, is going through his stuff and pauses over a half-eaten packet of gum, stops herself from throwing it out, and starts to cry. At this point, Sam, with sadness, but also disdain, rolls his eyes and says, "Molly, what are you doing?"

When I saw this movie after my dad passed away, this exchange made me angry. And then when I went through the same experience as my mother, I liked it even less. Who knows why things are important? Who is anyone to pass judgment on my mother or me for keeping something that may otherwise be insignificant? Everything is a memory. EVERYTHING. Even if you don't realize you made it … until that memory is all that is left.

A memory of what they liked and what they did. What they touched and the things they carried with them as they moved about the world. Molly could have been remembering a romantic garlic-laden dinner they shared, or how he never emptied his pockets before he put things in the hamper.

The truth is, she will be finding his stuff for years, and it will lose its raw significance, but not now. Not when the reminder that you lost someone is around every corner. Not when the pay stubs and the flyers and the slivers of soap and anything that was ever brought into the house by or for this person is now not going to be brought in or used by them anymore. Each one says, *I am not here to use this, and I am not coming back to get it.*

After the soul-crunching celebration of watching another movie that rips your heart out after you lose a spouse, please pause to remember this amazing actor, Patrick Swayze, and his widow, Lisa Niemi. Lisa, *The High-Flying Adventures of Captain Grief* salutes you! Your late husband is dearly missed, and he was the most beautiful drag queen *ever*!

WHEN GRIEF IS AWKWARD

"I went to a party last night," Captain Grief told me as we sat down to eat breakfast at McDonald's.

"So did I," I sniffled. I was sniffling because I noticed the green "Buy a Shamrock Shake" button on the cashier's vest and remembered how they were my wife's favourite every March.

I was biting into my muffin and about to take a sip of Earl Grey tea (which translates to one chocolate muffin, one tea, one sausage breakfast sandwich, one hash brown, and one juice), and I was going to ask, "Did you have fun?" But Captain Grief seemed a little more dishevelled than normal, if that were possible. She spluttered and spilled her tea.

"I took my cape to the dry cleaner's, brushed my teeth, and even wiped my boots on the doormat before I went in. I had a drink in my hand; I was feeling good and having fun! I hadn't been talking with this guy for five minutes before he asked me where my partner was."

"What did you say?" I asked, afraid.

"I told him my spouse was dead and he was a jackass; thank you very much for pouring lime juice in that gash. I threw a bowl of peanuts in his face and left the party."

I cringed.

She glared at me. "Well what am I supposed to say? Can that question *ever* have a response that won't totally trip people up or make them inch away or go glassy-eyed or suddenly need to go to the bathroom?"

I took a sip of tea to camouflage my cringe. "Maybe we could come up with a list of things to say (and do), so we'll be … better prepared."

"Fine … but I'm sticking near the snack foods in case they don't work."

Nine ways to follow up the sentence "My spouse died" to avoid food wasting (and being called a jerk)...

1. Uh, my spouse died ... but don't worry! I have a freezer stocked with single-portion leftovers, and I carry a puppy in my purse at all times.

2. Uh, my spouse died ... but don't worry about that really insensitive thing you just said; it hurt way less than actually losing my spouse. (Okay, that one will probably only make *you* feel better, but hey, sometimes that's what it's all about!)

3. Uh, my spouse died ... but I'm here and my family is here.

4. Uh, my spouse died ... but now I can use all her socks to make puppets for a puppet show that will make children all over the world giggle.

5. Uh, my spouse died ... but now I can sit on my front lawn and busk: "Put a penny in the can for the widow, Mama needs a new pair of shoes ... or maybe singing lessons."

6. Uh, my spouse died ... but now I can make room in the closet for a buttload of shoes.

7. Uh, my spouse died ... but now I can watch what I want on television (when my toddler is asleep) and eat junk (if I don't eat it in front of my toddler) and sleep in a star formation in the middle of the bed (if my toddler doesn't wake up and refuse to go back into his crib). Hmmm, how has my life changed?

8. Uh, my spouse died ... but now I can enjoy all the things in life that she was not a fan of. Like chick movies and chick flicks and period dramas that happen to have a lot of romance and drama — and a lot of ... chicks.

9. Uh, my spouse died ... but don't worry. I'm not on the couch in the same food-splattered, tear-stained pyjamas I've been wearing for seven weeks ... with takeout on speed dial ... where they don't even ask me for my name or order ... they just bring the grub. No! I'm up and groomed and talking to you. Aren't you impressed?

RETREAT, RETREAT!

I have a lot of little places in the city where I like to write. Pubs and coffee shops, libraries, and on my phone between stops on public transit. There's something about life humming all around me while I'm in my quiet bubble. I have an addiction to journals; they're where I write my best stuff. But sometimes I need more than just me and my words.

I started taking courses with my writing coach, Chris Kay Fraser, shortly after I met Kara. My first class was on writing memoir, and it was extraordinary to experience such a safe, intimate space to allow very real, raw writing to surface. She quoted a writer who basically said memoir is an act of brutal honesty. And it's true. Like all art, you have to search for the beating heart of something to find authenticity, and when it's memoir, it tends to go straight to the beating heart of you.

I started writing out the oral traditions of my family at our cabin on Manitoulin Island. Working with Chris, I found my voice, and as I told stories about my family, she and all the other students knew Kara as well as they knew me. I began attending her glorious writing retreats, which were always soulful, replenishing deep-cave diving for not-yet-expressed material.

On my first retreat after Kara died, I was all prepared to be one hot mess of a memoirist. When you go into silence and focus, you can't avoid what's there. It just empties onto the page, filling the vacuum. I definitely made a mess, but I also wrote like a fiend, and I was surprised to find that one of the deep, unexpressed things I needed to write about was joy — and where the joy connected to Kara first began.

Journal Entry

Damn that was a shitty apartment. Shitty and perfect. It was yours, and I found you on www.pinksofa.com, a lesbian dating site. I messaged you because I liked your handle, City Butch. You were riding past the Toronto Healing Arts Centre on Bloor and Christie the day we met. My client had cancelled, so you came back to meet me for lunch, even though you had just finished a night shift at the Toronto Island Water Plant, where you worked as an operator. *Clearly the Universe wants us to meet*, I thought.

I heard the door open downstairs. It could have been someone else, but I knew it wasn't. I was bent over, taking down the unused massage table, so the first thing you saw when you came upstairs was my butt. You're welcome.

You smiled your twinkly-eyed smile, and when I hugged you hello, the first thing I noticed was how incredibly warm you were. My furnace. The warmth was a gateway to my future, the temperature that I would come to expect for the rest of my life. You took me to Rocco's Plum Tomato for lunch, and after that you had to grab a cab back to the ferry dock, to catch the boat before your next shift. You normally rode your bike everywhere, even in the slushy, wintery streets of Toronto, but you had damaged one of your tires that day and had to take it in for repairs. *Clearly.*

I honestly didn't want to end our impromptu date, and I was going downtown to meet a friend anyway, so I didn't mind splitting a cab. You flagged one down and we sat in the back chatting, the endless stories already flowing between us. I casually touched your knee and imagined the fireworks exploding in your brain.

When we got to the corner, a second passed where we smiled a mirror image of clandestine knowing, and you pulled me in for the warmest most delicious first kiss I had ever experienced. At some point, I became aware that people driving across Front Street beside us were honking and cheering for the two chicks kissing on the sidewalk in the business district.

The kiss started to strain under our smiles as we laughed and parted. I was so in. I watched the back of you as you walked away, long beige cargo shorts, ringer t-shirt, baseball cap. I waited for a moment on impulse to see if you would turn around, and when you did, you didn't seem shocked at all to see me still standing there.

I couldn't stand it — the pull of estrogen was too potent. I spent the day with my friend in a giddy, bouncing mood, and met Kara again on the way back from her last shift to have the originally suggested date. After we hopped in another cab to her place, she gave me a tour of her basement apartment.

It was uncomplicated: Here is the garage. Here is the room with nothing in it except a loveseat and a scratchy pullout sofa. I would become accustomed to lying on that pullout, over sheets, in various states of undress. A sofa we ate dinner on, where she served me her famous mushroom gravy over roast pork, followed by strawberries dipped in melted chocolate Easter bunnies. This is where we later created homemade Christmas ornaments using cookie cutters and clay. Her present from me was a set of stars—one gold, one silver—with tiny snowmen on them, and two royal-blue hearts with an angelic figure on each, one labelled "Kelly" and one "Kara."

Continuing with the tour, we saw the hall, the minuscule kitchen, and to the left, a bathroom, unremarkable until I saw the beautiful claw-foot tub. It was like finding a hundred-dollar bill in the pages of a library book. I may have even rubbed my eyes to make sure it was real. Here was a person who was just as passionate as me about sitting up to the neck in vanilla-scented water. This was the person who swam next to me, lovingly, playfully towing me over the surfaces of Ontario lakes, as I gazed into the sky. I was with Kara, and I was home. The dingy grey carpet under my bare feet was parting to let my roots find their way into the ground.

When she stretched her arms around me, she smelled like damp earth and men's cologne. The gender of who she was and the way she dressed was cushioned by the soft female biology underneath. Kara was the mystery of how those two things came together. She was a perfect balance of a loving and nurturing internal strength, with a strong exterior that made my desires spill all over the floor like an unravelled ball of yarn. We had known each other for only one day and already we belonged to each other.

All my fears were gone.

CHANNELLING JUDITH VIORST

"So what are we doing here?" Captain Grief rolled her tear-filled eyes as she lay draped over the counter at Chapters. The March snow that had fallen onto her head during our walk here was melting down her face.

"I just need to pay for this book and then we can go." I showed her the copy of one of my favourite children's books, *Alexander and the Terrible, Horrible, No Good, Very Bad Day,* by Judith Viorst. I had a lot of favourites, as my mother was a primary school teacher, but I had not added this to my children's collection yet.

"Does your kid *really* need another book?" she asked. Not having a superkid of her own she didn't really get the value of a picture book when you have to explain why life sucks sometimes.

"Books are comforting. Just ask the shelves in my bedroom."

"Whatever. I need caffeine." Sitting down for a cup, the Captain picked up the book and leafed through it with an increasingly skeptical expression. "Gum in your hair? New running shoes, kissing on TV, railroad pyjamas! Sounds like a party; what is Alexander complaining about?!" That's when the couple next to us started staring, only infuriating her more.

"My best day is a hundred times worse than that!" she said. "Alexander wouldn't know what hit him!"

The couple discreetly asked for their cheque.

I looked at them apologetically, then snatched the picture book back and said through my teeth, "Alexander is prepubescent and hasn't lost a spouse."

"That's beside the point."

"Okay, what made your day so bad?" I offered, settling in for a long tale.

"Oh, where do I begin?"

CAPTAIN GRIEF AND THE TERRIBLE, HORRIBLE, NO GOOD, VERY BAD DAY

When Captain Grief woke up that morning she realized she had cried herself to sleep listening to sad songs on her iPod, again, and it was *dead*! She was also still wearing her cape, which was all wrinkled. While brushing her teeth, she missed the toothbrush and squeezed an aquamarine lump of toothpaste into the sink. After crying about the stupidity of life and squeezable tubes for ten minutes, she realized she didn't have the energy to clean up the toothpaste, so she spat into the sink and went downstairs to make toast. She knew it was going to be a terrible, horrible, no good, very bad day.

Emotionally exhausted by the toothpaste incident, she had to take public transit to work. On the way, she sat beside a woman on the subway who told her she looked like she needed a hug and tried to sell her a magazine subscription. When the Captain refused, the lady burst into tears. Captain Grief had no choice but to launch into a hysterical fit and shouted, "What! You think you can get a better sob on than me, over a freaking magazine? I'm Captain Grief! My spouse died and you are *so* less sad than me, you asshat."

That's when the lady pulled the emergency stop cord and they were both catapulted to the end of the car and into a catfight. The lady was an ear puller. They were escorted from the station. When the Captain trudged up to the surface, cradling her beet-red ear, she realized she was twenty-two stops away from where she needed to be and she had no money for a cab.

Now even more exhausted, she decided to walk. She was also wondering if her eardrum had blown because she was feeling all wonky. Although, lately she'd been experiencing unexplained, brief periods of nausea; motion sickness was now an Achilles heel and she carried a barf bag in her superbelt. The ear puller had also damaged her lunch bag, and her applesauce had begun to run down her leg through her tights until it dribbled into her boot, so she squelched on every other step.

"Yup, this is it," she mumbled. "A terrible, horrible, no good, very bad day in full effect. I think I might move to Switzerland where no one argues, or eats applesauce!"

Of course she was late, and when she arrived, sobbing and covered in applesauce, she threw a hissy fit at her boss because the soap dispensers were out of soap, and she was almost fired. Her cape got sucked into the shredder and she had to wait an hour and a half for the handyman to cut her out of it, since he assumed it was an additional call about the soap dispenser. Her computer was hacked and she received eighty-two emails about the trip for two to Switzerland she had won.

She got a huge paper cut on her thumb and the office shih tzu, Mr. Giggles, peed on the power bar and sparked a fire that burned the whole place down. As she left the smouldering building, she said to the handyman, "I hope they don't have terrible, horrible, no good, very bad days in Switzerland, 'cause I'm booking a flight outta here."

On the way home, she stopped at her favourite lesbian superhero bar for a drink, and a lady in a lime-green jumpsuit and hot-pink balaclava offered to buy her one, even though she was still smoking from the fire, so she figured, why not? After explaining the ashes in her hair and the absurdity of her day, she took off her gloves and reached for a pretzel. Super Jumpsuit Queen noticed her wedding ring and said, "Oh, you're married?"

"What's that supposed to mean?" Captain Grief blasted. "I can wear my ring as long as I want to! No, I'm not technically married anymore, but thanks for shaking salt over that wound, you jerkwad!" At this, Super Jumpsuit Queen smiled and backed out the door without breaking eye contact until she hit the pavement and pelted down the street.

The Captain mused, "Who knew this terrible, horrible, no good, very bad day could get any worse? I think I could have approached that better. Oh well, her loss." And she tossed back her drink.

On her way home, she realized she hadn't charged her iPod, so instead of listening to music, she thought about how shitty she felt and listened to the inner melody of her sorrow. She also forgot to stop and get tissues, so would be blowing her nose on the drapes again that night.

Maybe I'll order a pizza, she thought. *Then I'll have a box to put on the roof of the pizza box fort in the living room.* Smiling, she realized she felt the tiniest bit better, until she remembered they probably made better pizza in Switzerland.

WHERE SHE ISN'T...

March got me thinking about the spring and eventually moving on from where I was. I looked back at my January entry.

Journal Entry

I look at this house and it says you're not here. I look at the corner of the couch, the vegetable patch, the kitchen, the shed. They all say the same thing. They tell me I'm looking for you in all the places you are not, which is everywhere.

You're not behind the fridge door riffling for fresh dill and ginger and mustard. You're not cutting the grass or turning the delicately grill-marked chicken on the barbecue. You're not snoring upstairs. You're not on night shift. You're not putting the baby to bed.

You're not just beyond the reach of my fingertips or touching the small of my back. You're not taking turns with me in the narrow bathroom to brush our teeth. You don't even have a toothbrush here anymore. I threw it out because it hurt to stand there and look at it every morning and every night, in a bathroom that is suddenly too big.

The motions of living in this house, the dance of my daily life is a dance I do alone now, but you are still there. From the moment I get out of bed to when I crawl back to my room at night, I say things like, *Now I'm going to eat and it will be without Kara. Now I'm going to shop and I will shop without Kara. Now I will clean up the toys and feed the baby, fold laundry and watch a movie, without Kara.* Each activity carried out with the conscious awareness that you will have no part in it.

I know this doesn't go on forever. I did the same thing when my dad passed away. It's been fifteen years and the stitching over the tears in my daily life are part of the fabric. I am cut up much more infrequently than I was in the past, yet when the cut comes it severs. I would say, *I'm going to graduate, I'm going to get married, I'm going to have a baby and Dad will not be there.*

This is the fabric of loss, the blanket I clutch to myself just to hold something in my hand. It's the blanket I am left with, woven out of memories and grief and desire when the physical has passed. It's the blanket I spread over me at night that smells less like you with the passage of time, but it's what I've got.

It's the blanket I will wrap around our son like a shield when I think about the times when I will drive him to his first dance or his first job or his first year at university, without you. I will try to shield him, but nothing can cover the fact that you, his mama, was only in arms' reach for the first nineteen months of his life. I know there will be times when I can do nothing to ease his loss, because it is unfathomable.

But I will cover him and I will cover myself. When bedtime is as empty and cold as a lake in winter, when I wake and the jagged shards of my spirit lay glinting in the moonlight, splintered on my insides, when I try to breathe and they dig deeply into my flesh, I will lay the blanket on me. I will cover myself and remember the soft folds of your body, the way you rolled over to whisper and kiss me in the dark. To touch my face, to caress my hair and wrap your arms around me just to let me know you were there. It is then I will close my eyes and somehow I will say, *And now I will go to sleep. And it will be without Kara.*

I wrote that just before Captain Grief arrived, and even though there was a long way to go in the Year of Firsts, I think there was already some microcosmical movement forward. Let's call it a sign of hope.

CHAPTER TWO
I CAN CRY IF I WANT TO ... DAMN IT

"I don't like to be told what to do at the best of times," Captain Grief huffed as she sat frazzled in the front seat of our rental car. I had just watched her have an animated altercation with the parking attendant. She told him that, since there were spaces allocated for disabled individuals, expectant mothers, and people with children, there should be spots available for widows and anyone else who is grieving. She said he should mark it on with sidewalk chalk. Grumbling, we made our way toward the spot he suggested.

"Wouldn't that be nice." I smiled and thought of the possibilities. "I got dressed and dragged my ass out to this shopping mall, so I shouldn't have to drag my ass all the way across the parking lot after I park my car! If grief was like a walker, people might be jumping up to help me carry my emotional baggage. No wonder some people choose to wear black for a year. It's sounding more and more practical."

"Yeah, it sucks," said the Captain. "I'm emotionally sapped, incapable of forming a sentence, tired and aching and depressed and most likely sobbing, *and* I have to wander the parking lot for hours afterward, crying with my bags while searching for my car. Bloody injustice."

I shrugged as the Captain locked the car, and then we meandered toward the mall for new bedspreads. "At least there are a lot of sympathetic people who realize you're going through a tough time and deserve some allowances. And I don't know about you, but it makes me feel empowered to realize that I deserve them too. I'm allowed to do what I need to do to get through the grief!"

"Like what?" she asked.

And that's how we came up with the list.

Twelve things that would normally be frowned upon or misunderstood, but that you can get away with when your spouse dies...

1. I am allowed to eat Cheetos for breakfast.
2. I am allowed to bawl in the middle of an aisle at a grocery store and cause a grocery cart traffic jam.

3. I am allowed to forget to shower and not know or care that I'm wallowing in my own stink.
4. I am allowed to never change the bedsheets ever again from the ones where my spouse last slept. And to dig through the hamper for her laundry.
5. I am allowed to dump the entire contents of her side of the closet onto the bed and sleep in it like a dormouse in a nest of household fluff.
6. I am allowed to snap at telemarketers. Nothing freezes a cold call in its tracks like saying, "No you can't talk to her. She's dead!"
7. I am allowed to cancel plans at the last minute because I can't bear to get off the couch, hold a conversation, smile, or wear deodorant or a bra.
8. I am allowed to bitch about the bloody inconveniences of death. Like unpaid parking tickets. (FYI, they remain unpaid until you sell their car!)
9. I am allowed to call my mother at four a.m., crying and snotting into the phone because I am alone and my child is throwing his pacifier at me.
10. I am allowed to yell at inanimate objects, break plates, scream into pillows, and have unreasonable tantrums à la toddler.
11. I am allowed to make room for myself in the fridge and the pantry and the drawers and the medicine cabinet. To

play and dance and sing and drink (safely — unless you shouldn't!) and eat and forget that that the world is (or at least feels like) a piece of shit.

Speaking of which…

My wife and I listened to Tina Fey's book, *Bossy Pants*, on our iPod during one of our last road trips. Tina talks about a rubber stamp her father had that said "Bullshit," which he used to brand offending paperwork. When I went to Party City to get favours for my son's second birthday, I saw this large red battery-operated button with the word *Bullshit* on it. I immediately felt better. I pressed it and to my delight, it crooned, "Now that was grade-A bullshit!" I had to keep pressing it. Out came "If bullshit were money, you would be a millionaire!" And "Bullshit alert! Bullshit alert!" I put it in my cart on top of the loot-bag favours.

It was coincidental that I found something so vulgar and satisfying to punch, just when I had a fresh cause to be angry at the world. I was going on a road trip to my grandmother's, with my mom and my sister, Jackie. I had to tell my grandmother that my wife (whom she called my husband … she was 99, give her a break) had died, and on the way up there, all three of us had the this-is-so-hard-and-unfair grumps.

I was distraught over how to tell my grandmother, and I refused to do it over the phone. So, when we were on a call to arrange the visit, I had to pretend nothing had happened. I needed the Bullshit Button in my life. So to round out the list…

12. I'm allowed to … use this button and share its fertile blessings with the people in my life.

The night before we left, I decided to demonstrate the charms of the Bullshit Button to my mother — in the middle of a conversation, without warning her. I waited until she said something appropriately inappropriate and buzzed it at her. "What a crock of *bullshit*!"

She was stunned and horrified, until she wanted to punch it herself. I told her how I had a fantasy of carrying it around to meetings and letting this little jewel to speak any required response. You know, for those times where you're thinking, *If it gets any deeper in here, I'll need a ladder to climb out!*

My mother always said that grief is like wading through a pile of shit. You just have to keep going, and one day you look down and see the level of shit is at your navel instead of your armpits.

You may not be up to your eyeballs in it anymore, but hey, shit is shit. She fell in love with the button too. We sampled all the rude options a number of times so we could pick our favourites, and we settled on "Everybody put on your helmets, bullshit is being flung!"

I told you grief was messy…

WHEN ALIENS WEEP

"It's the big things that trip you up. Even though you can see them from a mile away. And sometimes it's the small things that you don't see coming that level you, because they're so minuscule." I was in a bit of a rant over these "small things."

The Captain was eyeing me warily as I sketched some sort of a line graph on the whiteboard propped up on my son's easel. I guess it was an attempt to show the explosive emotions of grief, how unpredictable they are, how they keep happening over and over. I wanted to understand it and really demonstrate how off-balance we can get when grieving. But I got so frustrated that I really just wanted to give grief the F-U.

"So we all know grief is messy, but let's look at the specifics. What's the real muck of the situation? How pathetic is pathetic?" I said to the Captain. "Things you find yourself doing when you're grieving might come as a surprise even to yourself, but that's the way poop flies. Isn't it?" I turned to look at her and saw an alarmingly offended expression on her face. I didn't see that coming. It made me want to cry.

"Are you calling me pathetic?" she seethed.

"No, no. You misunderstood. It's pathetic how small things can utterly destroy us when we're grieving. To the outside world, they may seem insignificant. I burst into tears in all sorts of situations that an outsider might look at and think were totally sad. And you know what, it *is* sad. Sometimes I cry and then I laugh at myself because it's ridiculous and unfair that such an itty-bitty thing can make me bawl like a baby, but that's where we are and that has to be fine because that's how it is!"

Her expression was still the hard, stubborn mask. "Are you calling me sad?" She crossed her arms and leaned on the kitchen table.

"Yes! You're sad. *We're* sad. We're *supposed* to be. We're *supposed* to cry at movie previews *and* the hole we made in our sock. We're *supposed* to howl when we forget the grocery list or have a hangnail or trip over the cat."

A glimmer of recognition crossed her face.

I sighed with relief and lowered my voice to an empathetic tone. "Processing grief is so heavy, so never ending, so all-consuming that it's the little stones on top of the boulder that trigger the avalanche." I wasn't surprised to see her tearing up.

"I had a cat once."

"What? Captain, you're missing the point." I sighed.

"*I am not!* It was one of the things that made me bawl this week!"

"Do tell." I turned my back on her, and the eraser squeaked as I cleaned off the whiteboard.

"Can I just give you a list?" She reached out for the marker I was still holding. I passed it to her and we traded spots. I guess lists make her feel better.

"Go for it."

"But before we do that, I want to tell you a joke." I could only answer her with silence. She ploughed on. "What's the only thing that would make crying worse when you're grieving?"

"I give up."

"Three eyes."

"Okay, that's funny." I felt a pleasant convulsing in my face that turned into a smile.

"Hey, don't laugh, that wasn't the punchline! I know some of those three-eyed alien widows, and it's horrible!"

"So … that wasn't a joke."

"No. Don't be so insensitive!"

"No. I mean that … ugh, never mind, sorry for my lack of … tact."

"Of course, they don't have it as bad as the widower with an extra nose."

"Uh, can I laugh at that?"

"No, you cruel heart. Here's my list."

Dumbfounded, I stood back while she began to mumble and write.

Eighteen pathetic things that made Captain Grief cry just this week…

1. Lost my favourite left sock.
2. Forgot to flush.
3. Postal worker told me to "Have a good day."
4. It rained.
5. Legs got tangled in the bedsheets.
6. Had to pay a library fine.
7. Power went out.
8. Got shampoo in my eye. ["Okay, that's a gimme," I said.]
9. Cape got caught on a tree branch while I was attempting to rescue a cat.
10. Cat scratched me when I brought it home.
11. Cat refused to share milk.
12. Spilled milk.
13. Dropped my cookie on the kitchen floor.
14. Found a dust bunny under the fridge when I reached for cookie.

15. Cat chased dust bunny.
16. I saved it, dressed it, named it, and sat it on the couch to watch a movie with me while I cried.
17. Cat ate dust bunny (formerly Henry).
18. Cat coughed up Henry and moved out.

When she finally turned around, she greeted an upturned eyebrow, a complete lack of empathy, and a resignedness that this conversation was going no further.

"Oh, how you suffer."

"Shut up."

REGRETS ABOUT GRANOLA

Morning at a writing retreat…

The lake on Georgian Bay was winking at me through the window in a myriad of soft sparks. A small bird skipped across the surface and glided into its watery nest. That was the only sound. I listened to the deep silence that I knew would stretch until lunchtime, allowing each of us to claim our slice of serenity and do whatever we needed to do to let words flow.

I claimed my piece of the rug to do some gentle yoga. The silence didn't scare me anymore. I had worried that I would fall apart, but instead my body was opening like a tiger lily, quiet but bursting with the colour needed to paint the day.

You are still here with me in the silence, I thought, *not washing me in the wake of your loss but asking me to pass the salt from across the breakfast table. You are moving into the flow of my day, whispering to me to take another warm boiled egg, one of Danette's "positive phrases" eggs, the one with "You are amazing" on it in her pretty, curving script. You told me to drink the puddle of milk in the bottom of my bowl, which was made sweet and spicy by Chris's homemade granola filled with pungent candied ginger, toasted almonds, and oats.*

Memory stirred as I dropped the Earl Grey teabag into the hot water. In my ear, I heard Kara shudder and say, "I wish you had made that granola." Maybe it was just the breakfast that brought it back. Maybe I felt guilty. I did.

Or maybe you are with me as I move into my day and can't help but sigh and express your regrets about it.

Journal Entry

You bought me a lovely Mason jar with a lid that sealed tightly, and I giggled at the subtlety of your hint, as it was still a cute joke between us. When you brought home all the ingredients, you were flat-out asking me, albeit passively. Perhaps we were both being passive about our desires, in our new roles as mothers. When you took out all the ingredients, chopped them up, and stored them back in their containers, it was helpful, but awkward. Pregnancy was a second honeymoon for us as we prepared and nested through the winter, whispering affection into my belly, laughing when he kicked so hard in the night that he woke you up, but not me. When we were on the flip side of labour, reality came crashing down on me, and in the wholly new landscape of childcare, I was bearing up reasonably well. But under the effort, I felt small and estranged from you.

Now you have passed, and I have daily conversations with you about all the things left unsaid: the distance between us, the rough transition to parenthood, the formidable task of me being the primary caregiver, the disagreements we had and the way we made each other feel. Granola was small potatoes. Still, *I wish I had made that goddamned granola.*

There are other regrets, of course, but in the moment, as you flutter around me at the retreat, this one really stings. All the while that I was being stubborn in my avoidance, the ingredients sat there in the pantry, carefully chopped into little cubes that were spiting me. Now I'm sad, not just because all the little packaged portions are still there, turning stale in their prolonged state of readiness. It's that you asked me to do something, and I was too tired, hurt, sad, overwhelmed, or irritated to do it.

Now there is a stabbing simplicity in my need to make peace with the ginger and walnuts and coconut that makes me want to take it all out and make a monument, not a meal. One that represents a way to say I'm sorry. Actually making granola with it, touching it, consuming it, and saying goodbye each time I take a bite, until it is all gone for good. But I'm not ready to endure more loss.

Listening to my thoughts as you were, you sadly nudged me, saying, "It can't sit in the cupboard forever. What if it goes bad?" Ugh. Practical, excruciating. There it is, something more painful than a slow disappearance ... saying goodbye all at once. "I know," I answered.

But I will never be okay with you being gone. Especially when we were just starting to become a couple again. I don't want to be okay with you being gone.

I want you here so I can do it right.

So I can make granola the first time you ask, with love and without hesitation or excuses.

I want you back here so I can make peace with the fact that our house was a mess, that our life was disorganized, that we were drowning in belongings we didn't want to give up, and that it was killing me inside.

Now purging and cleaning feels like a betrayal. There's less frustration, there's less pain, there's less conflict, but that has all been replaced with loss.

The fucking irony of it all, that I am remembering at the retreat right now, is how much I love granola, how much I wanted it, and how sorry I am that we let so many things stand in the way of our simple joys.

GRIEF BRAIN DOG-SITS

So I was thinking of a new list … The worst things to forget you're doing in the middle of a task because you're grieving. But Captain Grief was late. *If Ms. Thang would care to show up, I might get this list written!*

At that point, there was a bash at the back door and in her indecorous manner, Captain Grief shouted, "Open the damn door before I blow your house in!"

I stood back against the counter and watched her push her way into the house. I was shocked to see that she was covered from head to toe in very disgruntled looking cats that seemed to have trapped their claws in her supersuit.

"Uh…" I raised my hands. "They can't come in."

"No kidding. Give me a sec." She proceeded to pick the shell-shocked felines off herself one by one and unceremoniously scooted them out the door, with some *raaaaaares*, *meeeews*, and *hisssssses*, until they were all gone. "I hate cats," she said.

"No, you don't." I furrowed my brow at my superhero pal, who quite obviously had just saved the wretched beasts in bulk.

"I do now."

"Okay, I know you have a dog, but I didn't think you could object to a lesbian's other favourite pet."

"I was on my way here for something…"

"Uh, yeah, to write the list of things we start to do and…" I smirked.

"Forget? I forgot."

"You don't say."

"I just did." She looked confused. "I was on my way when I saw Scratchy the Cat Burglar luring a bunch of cats with a box of wind-up mice. I went in to save them and he pressed the panic button."

"He has a panic button?"

"It's just an expression." She rolled her eyes at my apparent ignorance. "No, he took out a water gun and sprayed me with a solution of cat nip and cayenne pepper." I was speechless. "It stung my eyes, and I kinda freaked." She looked as if she was going to burst into tears. Again. "Spice is my kryptonite."

For the sake of the writing I broke out the last piece of chocolate-fudge cake in the fridge, and once she had medicated a bit we returned to the other task at hand.

"So, off the top of your head, any things that you forget?"

The Captain wiped the chocolate smears off her face. "Uh, sure. I was frying up bacon for my BBLT once and—"

"B … BLT?"

"Yeah: bacon, banana, lettuce, and tomato. Haven't you heard of that?"

I shuddered as my horror of banana in any food but banana bread rose to the surface. "Noooooo, can't say I have."

"Hmmm, weird. Anyway, I was frying up the bacon, I was crying, *obviously*, and I went to the bathroom to blow my nose."

"And?"

"I was in there for an hour," she snorted in response.

"Bacon burned?"

"Smoked like a mother! The drapes still taste like pork."

My mouth dropped open, as I saw the very bizarre visual. "Taste … like pork?"

"Don't judge."

"Right, insensitive me. Okay, what else?"

"Poker."

"Excuse me?"

"I was playing poker with some friends and left to feed the meter. I suddenly remembered I needed air freshener and tissue, and thought I might as well grab a bite to eat while I was at it."

"Well, that doesn't sound too bad," I said.

"It wouldn't have been if I hadn't asked the dog I was sitting to play my hand."

"Oh dear."

"Yeah. When I got to the car, I remembered and went running back. By the time I broke up the game, I was down seven shoes (only the left ones), my newspaper, his new leash, and a fire hydrant he pried up from the sidewalk."

I tried not to laugh at her pain.

"Tell me about it. I'm still in proceedings for property damage and noise complaints."

"Wow. Anything else?"

"I forgot to lock the door."

"Whoops. Common. Not good, but not terrible either."

"I'll say. The dog got out and invited all his buddies back to chew the remotes. My toilet was dry, the fridge was empty, and I'm still finding *presents* ... everywhere."

"Crap," I said, with genuine sympathy.

"Exactly. Damn dogs."

"Okay, what about forgetting your cup of tea? Or dinner on the stove? Or dates with friends? Or leaving your keys in the door or a bath running?" I shuddered remembering that near-flood.

"Yup, yup, but nothing was as bad as walking away in the middle of a phone call."

"Oh. I hate the annoying high-pitched sound after the person you were talking to hangs up. I always scramble like mad to get back to the phone." (Only old folks like me, who had land lines, will remember this.) *Yes*, I thought, *now we're really on the same page with this list.*

"Ugh. I wish that was the problem."

Guess not then. "Oh?"

"Yeah … I made a call to Eloise's Super Psychic Network. I went to the door to accept a package. I'd ordered a new pair of super-hold walk-up-the-side-of-a-building boots, and when I came back inside, I was tired from interacting with people and I conked out on the couch."

"What happened?" I asked.

"Well, nothing. Until I woke up in the morning, poured my cereal, and noticed the phone off the hook." The Captain paused for effect and I waited in silence. "*They didn't hang up*. Said I owed them three thousand dollars, payable by credit card, for prime-time guidance."

"Ouch."

"It wasn't all bad. My services came with an aura-cleansing tea and a Merlin cap."

"Expensive hat."

"You better believe it."

"Is there anything else you can think of?"

"Oh yeah. Once I was ironing and—oh shit. Scratchy is back-y." She headed out the door, and I closed it behind her and waited until the sounds of the high-pitched battle ceased before I opened it again, wary of leftover cats.

"Captain? Caaaaptain? Oh well, we tried." *Hmmm, I'm hungry now*, I thought. *I think I'll make a BLAT (bacon, lettuce, avocado, and tomato sandwich).* And I'll *try* to remember not to forget about the bacon.

MY NEMESIS IS LEMON

I sat looking at my filing cabinet ... sighing. And *no*, not with any sense of disappointment, chagrin, or even slight heartburn. I was looking at it with a total sense of *satisfaction*.

I loved my wife, but what I did not love was her filing system. Did she use folders, staples, or paper clips to help her organize? No! Hell, I would have been happy with a Rolodex stuffed with clues as to where the life-altering information might be, but no. Instead Kara used ... piles.

Piles of paperwork to the left, piles of paperwork to the right, piles falling over other piles, getting mixed into the other less important/completely useless paperwork that we would have to constantly sift through and keep an eye on to access what we really needed. Example? Proof (or so I thought) that I was the beneficiary of her life insurance, which by some monumental cock-up, I wasn't.

That took a good six months to resolve. Just thinking of the lawyer bills makes me squeamish.

Anyway, where was I? Oh, paperwork! When she died, I inherited it all. I sat around cursing the Universe and screaming at it to bring her back, and I also cursed that I was now going to have to deal with all the piles myself.

However, rage burns out. And I realized I had a unique opportunity — and a fundamental right — to do everything the way I want to. Death is just so hard … sometimes I need to find the pluses so I can stay positive, or at least upright. I'm not ready to call them "perks" but I think it's okay that I like reorganizing the kitchen the way I want it to be.

Small things like this make some things easier in this horrid, putrid mess that we call grief.

I started by rearranging the furniture, hanging pictures, and going through bins of stuff to take to donation. At first I felt guilty, like I was constantly asking for permission or input when she was not there to give it. Then, as my house worked better for me and I started to be more comfortable with, and even proud of, my efforts, I began to experience something I hadn't felt in a long time. Happiness. Weird, huh?

The paperwork, however, was a major issue from the start. We had made the brutal mistake of putting off making a will. To add to that, when I went down to the basement to look through files and organize all the piles, I saw glaring gaps. I didn't have some of the records I needed (on top of a will), and I could only thank God that, living in Canada, she and I were legally married. In the chaos of missing paperwork and the discovery that my life was about to become a lot more difficult, I was incapacitated with doubt, fear, sheer panic, and an occasional urge to vomit. The only consolation I had was really cute Band-Aids.

Then my mom bought me a little purple plastic folder, wrote labels, and filed all the important documents in it. *I love you, Mom.* It was like taking a bite out of paperwork that was still a little sour but much more digestible. Slowly, painfully, we worked through what we had bitten off.

It took five months to get it all organized and then be brave enough to work through the rest of it. Somehow, I knew I was ready to look at the bags and boxes and satchels and chests filled with crap/really important items that needed to be relocated.

One night, about half a year into my loneliness, my son went to a babysitter and my mom came over and made tea while I sat on the floor and made piles until all the piles were gone. By the end, my hands were riddled with paper cuts (worst in the webs between my fingers), but it was all stored away neatly in a little black metal filing cabinet in my new office, which was originally the left side of the dining room. I lay on the barren carpet, the throbbing in my hands my badge of victory.

I was so overjoyed that I, the healer, didn't bother to treat my hands in any way but went about my day with a rosy glow, planning a barbeque for the next day. I am always better working to a deadline. Success is its own balm, I guess. In retrospect, it would have been good to look up curative applications in the moment. I did later Google it, with Captain Grief snickering in the background the whole time, and found this advice: After you wash your hands, put a drop of crazy glue on the paper cut to seal it (so long as you wait for it to dry before you go back to the paperwork) or use nail polish as a last resort. Or soak your hands in a cup of peppermint tea to soothe the inflammation and disinfect, or use some fresh aloe vera. *Note: Nowhere is lemon suggested, duh!*

When it was almost time for my guests to arrive, the Captain still wasn't there, even though she had promised to come early. In her absence, I was almost skipping on the way to the kitchen to grab the fresh produce that was awaiting utopia. I mixed olive oil, dill, *and lemon* in a bowl and began to massage the magic marinade into my veggies *with my bare hands.*

Son of bitch! The lemon stung as I tossed the barbecue-bound food, but it was a good sting, I guess; it was the sting of productivity. I felt in control of the main floor of my house. My son was turning two, and I knew that even though things still sucked, and I had not yet siphoned even the first few layers of water from my well of grief, I was going to be okay.

And then I paused to cry like an effing baby.

After a few minutes, I felt someone poke my side. Captain Grief had snuck in and was leaning casually against the door frame.

"Dude, you okay now?" Captain Grief produced a tissue. I glared at her, but took it nonetheless and blew my nose. "Good." She sighed and wiped her forehead melodramatically. "It would have been really boring making fun of you all by myself. You want to talk about the blog post?"

"Fine, you start."

"Okay," she chimed cheerily and continued in a condescending tone, reminiscent of a radio announcer or used-car salesman. "How about this? So, Kelly, I heard you were literally doing the backstroke in paperwork after your wife died. What did you do with it?"

"I filed it, you doorknob."

"Booorrring." She yawned.

"So what are *your* brilliant suggestions?"

"I have an idea for you." She paused for effect. "Round up every single little insipid scrap of paper telling you to fill this out, send this in, have this stamped, look through your records, confirm this, prove that, lick this — and put the detachable portion in the mail. Then collect all the leftovers, take them down to Cherry Beach, dig a pit, pour them in, and light the mother on fire!"

"Wow. That's … permanent." I'd left Irritationville and settled in the town of Incredulousness. "Don't you think it's good to file copies? It worked for me." I was thinking about the hours and hours Mom and I had put in, making my mess organized, understandable, and accessible.

Then I eyed her speculatively. "Hand over the matches."

"I have laser-beam eyes. Why the hell would I carry a matchbox?"

"Just hand it over."

She grumbled and dug a matchbox out of her utility belt and lobbed them at me. "Fine, but don't complain to me about your paper cuts!"

"Duly noted. Okay, so what about our readers who would like to keep the information but have no idea how to organize it? There's quite a lot, you know."

"No kidding." She started to pace the kitchen floor, listing inconveniences on her fingers. "You fill the damn stuff out, lick the horrid-tasting envelope adhesive — or peel and stick something that will not stick and has to be reinforced with scotch tape — buy stamps for the dingbats that don't provide postage, send it all away, and wait six to eight weeks for a response, only to get a snotty letter back saying they need more documents, more proof, more paperwork filled out … What was I talking about?"

"Suggestions on how to make use of—"

"Oh right, what to do with the damn stuff. Hmmm … decorations? Evil paper dolls strung like mistletoe in the front window so the postal workers take one look at them and never deliver another official-looking document to your house again?"

I got comfortable making tea as I knew she was going to be at this for a while. "Hmmm, well, that's one way to create additional problems. Earl Grey or chai?"

"Chamomile."

"Probably wise." I waited for an answer to the other question.

"Not good enough? Fine. How about insulation? Old houses always need more. And it's a kind of filing system that won't take up room!" Captain Grief suddenly beamed like she had achieved world peace.

"But it requires me to *open up the walls*." I handed her a mug.

"Well, losing someone is a pain in the ass. What do you expect from me?!"

"I guess that's fair. What about if you want to get it to the right people later, when you need it again?"

She looked at me for a moment like she was planning something evil. "The barbecue! They're already on their way! Use the paperwork" — she said this with a nasally, taunting voice — "to line the baskets for the burgers and fries. Martha Stewart would be so proud!"

I raised an eyebrow and handed her a plate of lemon-wafer cookies. She ate her cookie in smiley-eyed silence.

I set the plate down and faced her. "So now that you've had a bonfire, filed your important records in the walls for later use, and delivered all official forms to the correct government agencies and companies with a side of fries, how do you celebrate?"

"Simple." She took a giant gulp of her tea, put down the mug, and crossed her arms. "I crack open a cold one, collapse on your lawn chair, and order a fresh batch of your grilled, lemon-tossed veggies. Stupidity is always delicious grilled."

"I'm done talking to you."

"See ya!"

If I may, I would like to add that I love having arguments with myself. I always win!

CHAPTER THREE
THERE'S NOTHING WRONG WITH CAKE

Selfishness has gotten a bad rap over the years, especially where women are concerned. Sometimes it feels like guilt, shame, and the inability to say no is encoded in our DNA instead of socially constructed. Not *all* women of course. (If Captain Grief were here, she'd be rolling her eyes at me right now.) However, as she is a fictional character, I'd like to reiterate. Women and people of all genders experience self-consciousness, and there is no more inconvenient a time to have a case of the I'm-embarrassed-by-myself blues than when you're grieving.

It's kind of unavoidable, given that grieving is such an intense emotional process and the world is not always stellar at tolerating it. And even if they are tolerating it fine, you can do just as well shaming yourself about crying too loud, crying for too long, talking about your loved one constantly, or apologizing for yourself and the fact that you are *not getting over it*. Captain Grief said something about people who feel that way too, but I can't put in writing.

It's true. Death scares people, makes them uncomfortable, and causes them to question their own beliefs about mortality. And when you're grieving, you really don't have the energy to worry about other people; you just have to be honest. In order to cope, I adopted a sarcastic sense of humour about death and death-related topics to balance my lack of compassion. Incredibly, I had never heard of a case of literal "gallows humour" until I discovered the amazing writer Leslie Annis and her hilarious blog about her dead cat.

The poor guy croaked in the morning and she was forced to put him in the deep-freeze until she could tend to him. Then she forgot to tell her husband. This hits the nail dead centre, as far as I'm concerned. I've been labelled "a little morbid" at times, but really, what's morbid to some folks is reality to other people.

I get a kick out of the shocked look on people's faces when I break out the gallows humour. It's usually followed by a sigh of relief and then laughter. My wife died in November, and in April, I still had her box-shaped urn on the kitchen counter, on top of which was the small box containing our cat's ashes, who we had to put down a few months before Kara's death. It was literally a block tower of dead family members waiting for the spring thaw! Do I hear a gasp? I think it's hilarious to see how unnerved some people are when they aren't yet in a position to be candid about death. But that isn't the problem.

The problem is that when you stop yourself from grieving openly or you feel really apologetic about it, it only makes you feel worse.

Getting to the topic of cake, though, there is no proof that Marie Antoinette snubbed the hungry masses with her legendary phrase, "Let them eat cake." I bet she was not shy about treating herself well when she was having a rough go at court. Aristocratic and ignorant leanings notwithstanding, I not so humbly suggest you take a leaf out of Marie's book and say, "Let them eat cake." Or rather, "Let *me* eat cake!"

When you're grieving, do the things you need to do, go where you need to go, talk to the people who get it, and avoid the things you can't handle, until you can. If you have to buy a powdered wig and a corset and mow down a frosted baked good on the bad days, go ahead and do it. I can pretty much guarantee that Captain Grief is doing that right now. Well, I can do the cake, not the corset. Who needs that shit when you're eating cake?

I made a heart-shaped cake, broke it a little, and with very bad icing-manship wrote "Sorry about your spouse." Chocolate icing inside, butter cream outside (ugh — I didn't have enough chocolate icing because I ate some out of the can when I did my "I'm allowed to" list).

Going back to the tower of dead persons in my kitchen, some people were a little taken aback to see my wife's urn on the counter. Really, I think it's a perfect metaphor for how people respond to death, especially sudden death when the deceased is young.

It's shocking for death to appear in such an unexpected, common, and high-traffic location, like the kitchen counter. It's one of those things that just is. I came home from the funeral with a beautiful wooden box containing the ashes of my thirty-five-year-old wife, and I didn't know what to do. The chaos of arranging a service was over, and my new and suddenly glaringly real life without my wife bitch-slapped me in the face as I stood in our kitchen.

I was not going to be comfortable with this. But the question was, where would I be *least* uncomfortable leaving her urn? My wife was a phenomenal cook, and with roots in Cape Breton, she had a fondness for the kitchen party. Suddenly it occurred to me that I was already in the perfect place.

I'd spent a lot of time crying in our kitchen, especially when I was cooking her dishes for myself. When I was pregnant, she made me mushrooms on toast, and as I tried to duplicate her recipe, I couldn't see the frying pan through the wash of tears. I was sure I would never make anything that would be enough like hers to be comforting, but I was wrong. She always said, "Just cook, don't worry about making mistakes; throw shit in a pot. If the worst happens, order a pizza." So I kept at it and my atrophied cooking muscles grew stronger. I still can't ice a cake the way she could, but I am determined to have my ugly cake and eat it too!

THE QUEER WIDOWS/WIDOWERS CONVENTION

So you find the perfect partner and make a life with them, which possibly involves a U-Haul and probably a turkey baster, if you're a lesbian. (My wife and I got two for our wedding shower.) You commit to your partner any way you choose (or are legally permitted to) in your country. My sincerest and deepest condolences if it is not permitted in your circumstance.

So you're committed to one another in whatever form, and then ... BLAM! Your partner dies. *What the fuck do you do now?* Well, the same thing that heterosexual widows and widowers do when they lose their partners — grieve. The trouble is, when people have an issue validating your relationship, it can also mean they'll have trouble validating your grief. Captain Grief and I think that's a load of hooey. My way of protesting is to be loud, messy, and unapologetic about *my totally valid lesbian grief.*

The world needs to grow up and realize that love does not have a sex, gender, or orientation, nor does it have any specific religion, race, language, or culture. Love and commitment are gifts without strings attached, and no one segment of people has more right to them than any other. Of course, this is not an ideal world, so we must support initiatives for awareness and positive change. And while we're waiting for people to grow up, we dream. And this is what Captain Grief and I dreamt up one day:

Come one, come all, to…

The Queer Widows/Widowers Convention! A place to be with your fellow Queer Grievers and work through as many of the 7 Stages of Grief as possible. (Heterosexual Grievers with queer- and transgender-positive attitudes welcome.) These seven major installations follow the stages of grief, but they can be visited in any order, and each one can be experienced multiple times. Entry is free, and it's even more fun if you're adorned in rainbow apparel.

1. COMATOSE COFFEE HOUSE (SHOCK AND DENIAL)

This section of the Queer Widows/Widowers Convention (QWWC) is conveniently located at the entrance, as shock and denial is often the first stage of grief we experience. Kick back on one of our comfy couches and chat with new friends. You can all pretend this isn't even happening — that you're not at the QWWC — and you simply need a caffeine fix or you're waiting to see the dentist. If shock is more up your alley, feel free to stare blankly into space for as long as you want. For your convenience, we have walls and ceilings that come in a variety of patterns and colours, so you won't be bored to tears — that comes later.

2. THE GUILT GAUNTLET (PAIN AND GUILT)

If you're not sure what this is like, try running on a treadmill with sneakers that don't fit, shovelling snow in a giant walk-in freezer, or getting that root canal you've been putting off. If you need a more emotional kind of pain, there's a lending library with books, CDs, and movies guaranteed to make you bawl. "Enjoy" them in private or semiprivate rooms stocked with complimentary popcorn and soft drinks. Feel free to use the chalkboards to write down the things you feel guilty about. Just be sure to wipe them clean before you leave. And please clap the erasers!

3. THE BARGAINING BAZAAR (ANGER AND BARGAINING)

Picture a country fair where everyone is aggravated. Take a whirl at our plate-smashing booth, wrestle someone in a sumo suit (no biting), play a round of "A Million and One Things to Do with a Golf Club (That Are Not Golf!)," or take a stroll through "Sledgehammer City." I've convinced Captain Grief to sit in the dunk tank, as she'll likely be crying her face off and soaking wet anyway. If a good bargain is all you need, feel free to place a bid at our really loud auction, or peruse our garage sale and heckle to your heart's content. Staff members accept tears and irrational pleading as payment but also appreciate tips.

4. BLEEDING HEART CAFE (DEPRESSION AND LONELINESS)

This is, despite the title, the most comfortable section of the conference. When you're at this stage, make sure you have lots of support. Imagine this: hot tubs, mud baths, free massages, bereavement therapy, a napping tent, as well as yoga and meditation classes. Feel the need to express yourself? Use our art supplies, craft tables, and musical instruments. Be sure to take advantage of the open mic, and don't miss out on the regular performances of the Beatnik Poets Society, depressed artists that compose a fresh set of poems about death every hour, on the hour. Also, as a special treat, Captain Grief's grandmother has offered her services at the café. Get a table and enjoy some of Grandma Pearl's comfort cooking. If you need a complimentary hug, she's the one in the violet apron and cape. Her meatloaf and peach pie are truly super!

5. UPWARDS TURN ANNEX (UPWARDS TURN)

Simply a flight of stairs lined with encouraging posters. The other side of the stairs (which you may occasionally trudge back down) is lined with pamphlets on self-acceptance and self-forgiveness.

6. RECONSTRUCTION ZONE (RECONSTRUCTION)

This floor is massive and houses little cubicles with professionals of all varieties you may want to consult with as you develop your five-year plan. Also, there are lots and lots of water coolers. Sign up and rehydrate while you wait to see a lawyer, banker, doctor, dentist (a different one, if you went for the root canal option above), general contractor, gardener, life coach, motivational speaker, therapist, spiritual representative, government official, or employment agency assistant. Paper, pens, clipboards, and filing folders are all provided.

7. CLUB ACCEPTANCE (ACCEPTANCE)

Now we party! Come on up to the rooftop patio and enjoy our heated pool, lounge chairs, blow-up palm trees, live music (featuring the bluegrass tribute band famous for their cover of "Don't You Monkey 'Round My Widder When I'm Gone"), large dance floor, free bluegrass skirts, and an open bar serving a rotating selection of Jell-O shots and veggie burgers. A photo booth is also available (smiles and smirks preferred). Take a dance class and learn the mambo or the "Ha-ha-ha, I Made It! Hokey Pokey." Even though you've already learned that you're not alone, take the time to see what good company you're in, because that's what it's all about!

CAPITAN GRIEF VS. SWEET TOOTH

"Wow!" I took in a view of Captain Grief as I opened the front door. She was looking even more ragged than usual. Her outfit was tattered and smeared with what looked like wet sand, grease, and mud. Her cape seemed to have bites taken out of it, and her hair was standing up in places, as if she'd been through a wind tunnel while simultaneously having a fight with her firm-hold hair gel.

"Rough day at the office?" I asked.

She eyed me with disdain and grumbled as she shook herself out and sat down on the couch.

I turned on the kettle. "So, what happened?"

"Uh, Sweet Tooth attacked me on the way to the dentist. He hasn't forgiven me for stringing him up with my superfloss alongside the geese at the Eaton Centre."

I looked at the beach that was now on my carpet and sighed. That's what you get when you're friends with a superhero.

I shrugged. "I could see that." I handed her a mug of tea. "I have a lot of showdowns with him. I'm glad you finally taught him a lesson."

"Me too." She cringed as she picked a feather out of her ear. "But he'll come back."

"I know. He always does." I sighed.

"No, really, I'm expecting him anytime. That gumball machine won't hold him for long," she clarified.

"Thanks." I sipped my tea and waited for an opportunity to throw her out before the Master of Tooth Decay came banging on my door. Superhero friends.

"So," she said, eyeing me, "you're suddenly looking a little more … depressed. You riding a low at the moment?"

I smirked. "Thanks for noticing."

"Come on, what's up?"

"Well, since *you* mention it, I've been having a lot of showdowns with Sweet Tooth, and I'm getting sick of losing and beating *myself* up. Chocolate is addictive at the best of times, but when you're grieving…"

"Look out!"

"Exactly."

"No, look out!" the Captain shouted and pointed out the front window.

At that moment, a giant blob of gingivitis hit my side window. Captain Grief jammed me under the coffee table and ran out the door screaming, "All right, you bastard, I'm grieving! And your treats are like a sugary spit in the eye. You're going into the gumball machine for good!"

Journal Entry

I have a secret. A shameful, self-indulgent nobody-knows-about-it, need-my-fix secret. Not that you can't guess what it is, but I've been feeling pretty dirty about it. I do it behind kitchen cupboards when no one is looking, in dark movie theatres, before I go to bed, and anytime I want to. It's the luxury I've decided not to worry about in my first couple of months of grief.

I'd say I feel like Carrie Bradshaw, in my sweet, chocolatey, covert self-indulgence, if it were not so commonplace. Perhaps it's the giant box of Turtles I keep stashed in my underwear drawer causing this dirty feeling of guilt and shame. Sure, everyone likes sugar, and chocolate in particular, but I have a serious addiction. I have a carton of the most amazing chocolate ice cream in the freezer right now, and I think about it every time I walk past it. I have to do something about it.

You'd think I'm talking about narcotics or alcohol the way I'm going on, but I think sugar is a valid candidate for a gateway drug that can trigger all kinds of not-so-positive habits. I know how I am. The first time my wife and I went off sugar we were in line at a Tim Horton's drive-thru. *The poor woman only wanted a coffee and I nearly killed her to get to a doughnut.*

You know, sugar — and for me, chocolate especially — is instantaneous bliss, but now it's even more dangerous! Talk about needing immediate comfort and familiarity. The Captain is right when she says that's how Sweet Tooth takes advantage of us widows, scattering his treats like a trail of toxic cupcakes. I'm glad she's around to defend us against the likes of him, especially when I've got my own supervillains to fight.

Screw the withdrawal, I thought after I returned from a day of detoxifying spa treatments and hydrotherapy with my sister-in-law. I had experienced a rare but valid moment where I didn't need chocolate, so I decided, that's it. That's the line between immediate comfort that makes you feel like shit later and necessary deprivation that makes you feel like shit now but eventually leads to the realization that if you don't take care of yourself, you'll never feel better. And I assumed the weight would start to come off, especially since I was already following a strict diet of stress and chasing a toddler, although that wasn't really a long-term plan.

I spent the next hour waist-deep in cleaning products, leftovers, and old takeout containers, but eventually my refrigerator looked like a much healthier version of me lived here. All shelf-stable contraband was neatly packed away in a high cupboard where my short-ass self couldn't reach it. Instead, I would be feasting on yogurt and grainy breads, hummus, eggs, vegetables, fruits, and mostly lean meat for six days a week. No pop, no chips, no chocolate.

I mean, why make the commitment to exercise and stay away from the corner store while shoving chocolates in my gob? Why fight my insane urge not to sleep while drinking sodas to keep me alert, get more things done, and feel in control? *I don't like bedtime anyway*, I thought. *Nighttime is the worst part of the day. Who cares that I'm running myself into the ground.*

Well lots of people cared, actually. And one of them spoke very strongly one night. I was going through some old journals and came across the motivational flash cards my wife wrote me for when I went into labour, in case she couldn't get back from work in time. One of them said, "You are STRONG. You CAN do ANYTHING!"

In that moment, I got it. *I owe it to her simply because I owe it to myself.* She loved me and wanted me to be strong.

Now I understand that life does eventually get better. I had a right to stand in my own way — until not taking care of myself made it so much worse.

Taking care of myself became something I did for both of us. *I'll do it for her*, I thought, *as a way of saying "I love you" right back.*

Journal Entry

Well the grace period is over folks. Captain Grief is holding the record for the most incensed superhero ever. She's not taking my phone calls and I think she left that bag of shit in my mailbox the other day. Jerk. She's entitled, I guess, as she is grieving too — I just wish she hadn't said it with poop...

It all started when I mentioned that I wanted to feature my son in a blog post, especially as I was also doing a post about my mom the next week. I was going on and on about how proud I was of him, so I didn't see the steam coming out of her ears until it was too late. I think she was actually jealous of him. She didn't have a kid underfoot to make her smile every day.

So I would like to tell you more about the smallest person in my life, who helped me on a daily basis, simply by being himself: my Super Baby Boy. I love that my wife taught him how to make amusing cow, lion, and elephant noises on command. They will always be a part of him.

This leads me to the reality of grieving when you're a mom or dad. First you lose your spouse, the one you wanted to be with until you were old and grey and had parts dangling off you that didn't dangle in your thirties. Then you're suddenly a single parent. Alone to experience the fun and the milestones. Alone to make the decision of how to discipline, when to potty train, and how to go about life as two, not three. Alone, so you can't roll over after a cry in the night and say, "It's your turn" or "He's your kid" or "He doesn't get that from me."

I've told many people this would be so different if I weren't a parent; that I don't know how I would be if I didn't have my son (the best and most beautiful result of my relationship with my spouse). Grieving parents have a different type of challenge, especially if their child, like mine, is still totally dependent on them. Yet there is a different type of joy available to you if you have that motivation to pull it together for your kids. I was out of reckoning for some time, going through the motions of our routine but without any heart or attachment.

Things changed about five months after Kara had passed, and Ben and I were alone for the day. My little Ginger Menace was building roads out of blocks on the carpet, following them with his collection of cars, and making vrooming sounds.

I sat down next to him on the rug to watch and, without thinking, I picked up a shiny blue truck and vroomed down a road myself. All of a sudden, his car crashed into the side of mine; he cut me off and mowed my truck into the ground. Without thinking about it, I shouted, "Hey!" and laughed. Then I stopped, stunned, listening to the echo of my joy in the quiet house, and a slow smile crept to my face, like dry clay cracking in the rain and returning to its natural softness. My face felt like it was mine again. It was then that I knew I was going to have the opportunity — the capacity — to be okay.

It gave me the energy to plan a kick-ass Thomas the Train party for his second birthday, and a reason to gather my friends and family in the house. Their noise and laughter blew out the emotional cobwebs, so to speak. And for my effort, my son even blew out the candle on his cake perfectly.

It occurs to me that this was such a pure moment of joy I got to experience because I had a child. I thought about my childless friends and if they found themselves in my position. How would they find similar joy to distract them? I guess when you don't have kids in your life, you might volunteer with Big Brothers or Sisters or hang out with the kids of siblings or cousins.

Back to living with a child while grieving… When you're sharing a house and you're both grieving, you have to learn how to interact with each other, how to live with the grief *and* with the other person's coping mechanisms. My son spent the first month watching *Cars, Cars 2*, and *Mater's Tall Tales* — *his* coping strategy, so I could not take it away until he seemed not to need it as much. (This is why they were finally all hidden in the kitchen cupboard with the rest of the movies Mommy was sick of — *my* coping strategy.)

If the Ginger Menace could write a guide for kids about how to survive this, here is how it would go:

A Toddler's Guide to Surviving a Grieving Parent

1. **Watch your favourite movie on loop** for three to four weeks and bawl your face off if it goes away. When it's playing, sit calmly and attentively with your parent and favourite comfort item. You can get away with it, and they need the one-on-one time. The popcorn doesn't suck either.
2. **Make your parent dance** to the musical numbers. They need a distraction and they'll pull through for the moment.
3. **Pee through your diaper and sound the alarm**. This works perfectly for emergency nighttime cuddles. They may even let you sleep in the big bed.
4. **Do something brilliant.** Say a new word, do a new sign, make a new animal sound. Folks will be so delighted they'll forget all about grief — for a few minutes.
5. **Help around the house**. Parents like to feel that you're picking things up. Put away a few toys (after you dump the whole bin on the carpet, of course), eat a few mouthfuls before you chuck your plate, "fold" the laundry, "feed" the cat, stir the pot, and do what you're told to for long enough that they can function (and you won't have to make a serious commitment to obedience).

6. **Giggle at them** until they giggle back.
7. **Bring them something to eat** — and not something that has already been in your mouth. They won't think prechewing is a kindness; it'll be taken, but not appreciated. After they eat, they'll at least have more energy to say, "Someone take this kid to the park."
8. **Run and give them a hug** when you hear your parent cry. There will be ample opportunities, and you'll feel better too.
9. **Catch a cold**. Go lick a neighbourhood kid and run right home to kiss your parent. If they get sick and you get sick, they'll have to stay home and nurture you. This will release you from all the above obligations except the first, so go get the popcorn!
10. **Build a fort on the couch** when you're better and play a few rounds of peek-a-boo. If you lure them close enough, insist they join you, or at least whack them right in the face with a pillow when they don't expect it.
11. **Play the "really bad day" card**. Let the mayhem begin! Flush your soother down the toilet and empty the sock drawers. Take your parent's iPhone and order the entire Disney Classic collection on Amazon. These things may not appeal to your parent, but you need to let loose, especially after all the hard work you've done taking care of them.

CHAPTER FOUR

FEELING SORRY FOR YOURSELF... IS ACTUALLY A STAGE

The official Mother's Day was a write-off for me in 2013. Four days later, I decided, *Today is Mother's Day because I am celebrating* my *mother.*

I was catatonic on the couch for most of the day, nibbling at chocolate biscuits, drinking tea, and switching between staring out the window and watching one of my comfort movies. (Before you ask, my favourite is *Chocolat*, with Juliette Binoche, Johnny Depp, Judi Dench, and Lena Olin.) As epic a defeat as my rematch with Sweet Tooth was (Captain Grief was kicking his ass as I watched my movie), that is not what this is about. (Though I *was* grateful that the Captain had something to distract her from being pissed at me.)

There are not a ton of things that make grief an easier road to walk. Empathy and understanding are great. Having someone in your life who is also grieving can be helpful. And if that someone has lost a spouse like you, you'll have more understanding. But it's even better when that someone *is your mom.*

Mom, this list is for you!

Eleven reasons why it's easier to grieve the loss of your spouse when your mom is a widow...

1. She will edit your writing on losing a spouse with not only her educated opinion but a true sense of empathy. (The fact that mine is also a teacher and can correct my horrid spelling is an added bonus.)

2. When you're raking your hair out and crying to the heavens in vain, saying, "How do I do this, how do I do this?!" she has an answer, because she did it.

3. When you're raking your hair out and crying to the heavens in vain at four in the morning, you can still call her, and have her tell you again.

4. If you can't face the day, she'll come to your rescue with clipboards, lists, and groceries, or take care of your kid so you can go to bed because she knows how important that is. Mine loves spending time with the Ginger Menace, so I don't feel too bad, but I make sure I take her out once in a while to thank her!

5. And when it comes to advice about single parenting after your spouse has died, she has it in the bag!

6. She has ready-made gallows humour that the two of you already actively engage in, since her partner died — not only is it raring to go, but it's familiar and comforting!

7. She makes the best comfort food, so your tummy will be happy to see her. And when she puts her arms around you, you can fall apart for hours if you need to.

8. There's no cap on the number of times she will say, "It gets better." In the same way she knows that there's no cap on the number of times you'll need to hear it.

9. When you get to spend time with her (when you're not on the phone or standing in line or filling out paperwork or entertaining your toddler) she'll take you out and gladly share fries and a gin and tonic. And it will feel like you can breathe and that things are some semblance of normal again.

10. She'll show you it's okay to lose your temper, your patience, your mind, and your shit, and then she'll show you how to come back from it.

11. You can borrow her collection of bawl-your-face-off books and movies.

12. When you feel like your soul is in tatters and you'll never be happy again, you can look at her proudly and know that she is a shining example of how that is just not true.

I love you, Mom. Thank you so much for making this horrid, unbearable thing better.

SHRINES ARE FINE

Remembering has a number of degrees, and all of them are fine, provided no one gets hurt and you don't risk being carted off to the clinic. Really, they have to be fine because when your spouse dies, it feels like everything is a shrine. Places that you went, songs you sang, times of the day or week or month or year when something special or commonplace or horrible happened. They sit there, unchanging and as immovable as a mantelpiece.

This is especially so in your own house because everything in it will take on a new significance. This is why it's okay to keep it exactly the same, totally change it, hole up in it, or escape from it as needed.

One day, when I was rummaging through the basement for extra frames, I found an oil-pastel drawing I did for my wife for Christmas 2009. I put it up to fill an empty space, claim my first wall, and feel like she was with me, all at the same time. I call it Centre of My Life. It reads, "When I look at you. I see. The strong, warm centre. Of my life."

When my wife died, I could not stand being in my bedroom, and bedtime sucked. So I moved furniture, changed linens, and cleaned out her side of the closet. Once I had taken her out, I realized I needed to put her back in, in a way that was more comforting for me. *And with a big dose of girly.*

I found some beautiful pictures of her and framed them. My dresser became an altar, and a huge collection of pictures curling up the wall along the stairway was like a shrine to our life together. I created and bought new pieces of art that made me happy and brave, and reminded me I was allowed to take care of myself. In short, I made a sanctuary, and my wife's beautiful face was the star.

Captain Grief, on the other hand, took her remembering to superhero extreme! (She always was a bit competitive.)

Where I made a small collage with magazine clippings, Captain Grief ... well, I don't know if you saw the giant collage of pictures of her spouse she pasted over a billboard advertising soup? Yeah, the one on the highway. That was her. She was going to be charged with vandalism until her mom (Super Mom) explained the situation to the Superhero court, and relocated her art.

I made mashed potatoes with Kara's mushroom gravy for company. The Captain made a giant sand sculpture in the image of her spouse at the beach, but this used all the sand and she was forced to put it back when she was done. She then made smaller versions out of cornflakes and hoisted them up to the roof of her secret headquarters. When I pointed out that she wasn't very stealthy, she told me to screw off. Fair enough.

I belted out our favourite Melissa Etheridge songs with the windows open. But the Captain? Her biggest, loudest, most unapologetic way to pay tribute to her lost spouse was at a giant landmark. She solicited a crowd of businesspeople on Front Street and airlifted them into an empty SkyDome for a concert, starring her. She brought in cheerleaders and sold hot dogs and beer. When she sat on the Jumbotron and sang a karaoke mix of heartache songs, people cried and sang along. And before you ask about it: Celine Dion's "My Heart Will Go On"? Yes, she totally went there…

I guess this book is my Jumbotron equivalent.

BREAKNECK LEARNING CURVE

So this is how the magic happened. I may have conquered only a small domestic duty, but it shall not go uncelebrated. Captain Grief was off using her laser vision to explode stuff in space at the time, so I could stay home and write about it — the magic stuff, not the explosive stuff. I officially found my way around a small problem. Small in terms of detail, but ginormous in terms of things that were vital to live a (more) peaceful existence with a wilful child.

The Ginger Menace had some pretty profound meltdowns. And during one particularly hard week, many of those tantrums involved a set of children's nail clippers. Now you may be wondering how nail clippers might lead to WWIII in my house. He needed his nails cut, but almost nothing sparks a fire in a little Aries, Irish redheaded toddler than the idea of having his feet groomed. With a reflexologist as a mother, I figured our little man could enjoy the best foot massages in the neighbourhood. Turns out, what adults think is relaxing is … well really different from what a toddler appreciates.

This wouldn't have been such a big deal, except that I was dealing with an acute case of so-you're-suddenly-a-single-mom-itus. Every decision I made for the first time, or for the first time alone, was like nails on a chalkboard. A learning curve like this must be approached gently, even though it happens at a breakneck pace.

Without my wife, I knew I needed to butch it up, and if you'd ever met her, you'd know it's a formidable task to fill her boots. It's not that I was in any way incapable of mowing the lawn, using the barbecue, or calling her father when my washing machine began to smoke. It's just that with a partner, your life falls into predominant patterns based on comfort, habit, or preference, and my wife had taken over some tasks.

For instance, we had two cats. Piper despised her — yeah, you know the one who sat for months in a box in the kitchen, on top of my wife's urn? I must admit it still gives me a giggle to picture him sitting on her head, swiping at her from the afterlife for old time's sake. Piper didn't much like anyone apart from me, so while I clipped him, it fell to Kara to groom our other cat, Riley. However, since my wife and the uppity cat had both gone to their graves, it was now all on me to groom Riley (aka, Super Ginger Kitty, if you can believe it). Riley was not happy with this arrangement. Usually he would lie as limp as a noodle in my wife's sturdy embrace and fall silent when she admonished him for the slightest protestation with a smart, "Shhhht." When I did it, he made a perpetual high-pitched whine, somewhere between clammy hands squeaking on glass and an air-raid siren.

However, when I took him to the vet, I learned that *he was playing me like a tiny feral violin.* I was astonished as the vet showed me the actual location of the quick on his paws, and assured me I had not, in fact, cut past them and into nerve endings. Then he demonstrated by snipping all of them off in less than ten seconds. Riley looked at me as if to say, "What?" Me, one; Super Ginger Kitty, zero. It was a whole other story when it came to my whiney human baby … sort of.

Shortly after my wife died, I experienced a regular occurrence of panic when I thought about facing life's big and small challenges without her. I then hyperventilated a bit when I tried to actually face them. I was breathing well when I showed the Ginger Menace how Mommy cut her own nails, and he willingly offered up his little finger for the same treatment. Success number one. Then I clipped his flesh *just a little* and he pulled his finger smartly back — previous success obliterated. There was only a tiny amount of blood, but I lay wheezing with sobs on the bed for about ten minutes before I was brave enough to attempt it again, by which time it was a no-go.

I went back to biting off his fingernails when they were long enough, like I did when he was a baby, but the toes were getting ridiculous, and I wasn't about to put my face anywhere near his feet. That said, action needed to be taken. He had recently regressed to falling asleep in my bed, and he was not only kicking me but also stabbing my legs with his razor nails. I made a few more attempts to restrain his flailing limbs, to no avail. There is only so much crying a mom with so-you're-suddenly-a-single-mom-itus can handle.

A friend said to me, "Cut them while he's asleep." That seemed reasonable and in line with the path of least resistance. But I didn't want to turn on the light and risk waking him. That, and I was still so exhausted at naptime, I would go comatose and not open my eyes until he was in my face saying, "Wake up, wake up!"

After the fourth night in a row of hauling him into my bed when he started screaming somewhere between nine and ten at night, I woke up with a start at eleven and knew the time had come. After an hour or so of him cradling in the crook of my right elbow, I saw he had flipped over, gone diagonal, and fallen asleep with a pillow under his abdomen. *I can do this.*

I put on my wife's headlamp (I needed both my hands) and clicked it on. I reached for the clippers on the bedside table. Tentatively, I took his left foot and flipped it up so I could see the most offensive nail. It was jagged from my past attempts. I lined up the clippers. Snip. He didn't move. I breathed. Snip. First toe, done. He jumped and thrashed during the second toe, and I froze for a moment, then charged ahead. I got both feet done and, feeling a surge of confidence, decided I might as well go for it. When I did his hands, he didn't even move.

At almost one a.m., my bed was full of nail clippings, but I felt euphoric. I put the Ginger Menace back in his crib, swept up, and had a peaceful night. It was one more thing that proved to me: *I can do this alone.*

Next on the agenda was perfectly grilled slices of eggplant and chopping down the jungle that was my lawn. At least I wouldn't have to wait until it was asleep.

TODDLER COPING STYLES

Everyone's loss is different. Everyone's relationship is different. Everyone's route to healing is different. But what do you do if you are say … two years old? I am, of course, thinking of my son. Ben was not even two when my wife died, and it was really hard to explain this massive loss in his life.

He still waved at photographs and responded when I said her name. But I saw a change in him. By that first August, he was settling down to a new way of life, but for a while it was hell in a sand bucket. I didn't know what he was going to need or, equally, what I would be able to give him other than the obvious extra love and comfort. He needed it on the days when he was screaming and didn't want me near him. I think he was just frustrated and acting out his confusion and sorrow about the change in his life he couldn't understand … just like what my doctor and the books say.

The only way that children as young as Ben can process such a terrible loss is to regress. *So regress we did.* Eating habits demolished, bedtime rituals out the window, and the "okay, okay, you can have whatever you want" rule in place. Surviving those couple of months after catastrophic change is no picnic, particularly because you're deep in your own grief as well and fighting to just get through the day. So how does a parent do it? How do you grieve with your kids? Well, obviously, a huge dose of compassion for yourself and for them is vital, but exactly what helped us? Here's a list I imagine my little guy must have had to help us through:

What to Do after Your Mommy or Daddy Dies...

1. Demand pizza for dinner. And do it a lot. Sounds bad, I know, but when the pity casseroles run out, all your parent can do is dial the number and stumble to the door anyway.
2. Bath = romp in sprinkler. Sure, it won't work in the winter, but then you can use the sink. It'll be fun, for you at least.
3. Watch a movie on your parent's phone every night until you fall asleep. Screw the crib. Your parent needs the extra cuddles anyway.
4. Run sugared laps around the living room until you conk out. Your parent may be right behind you.
5. Pull the house apart. Take all clothing out of the drawers, all pots out of the cupboards, and all shoes and coats out of the front closet. Your parent needs to go through things for donation anyway.
6. Throw a fit. Pitch things pell-mell about the room until you're wheezing on the floor. Go right ahead, and don't mind if your parent joins you. [Parents: Kids need to see you cry too.]
7. Make more brilliant discoveries. Try climbing the bookshelf, scaling the side of the crib, feeding yourself

(which loosely translates to decorating your face with dinner), saying your first word, or trying to pick up the cat. These would be normal achievements, but your now-single parent will have to deter or celebrate as needed, alone, and then grieve.

8. Dress your parent. Those stripes may not work with those polka dots, but trust me, your parent will be much happier on the road if they let you have some small opportunities for control.

9. Have a massive birthday party. You all need to celebrate and have support around you the first time there's a birthday without the other parent. [Parents: Go all out!]

10. Demand a fun activity and be unruly until you get it. Play with play dough, "help" your parent bake banana bread, build a popsicle-stick house, make flubber, or create a play with puppets. You have to distract them. [Parents: Fake it till you make it! You could be just one activity away from a genuine smile.]

11. If all else fails, poke your parent in the eye. Not ideal, but it will get their attention. There will be a lot of crying (trust me your parent needs to) and you'll have to say sorry, behave yourself, *and not repeat any toilet talk*, but then — and here's the kicker — say, "Don't worry, it's okay to cry."

SHE CAN BE TAUGHT

So Captain Grief and I were thinking, well in advance, about our birthday blog post and what we were going to call it. We were thinking something like "Birthdays Blow ... My Candles Out" or "Birthdays Bite My Ass." Birthdays are the same as all the other yearly events that make painful memories rise from the grave. Perhaps that's why we did so much planning, though you'll see that it wasn't necessary as we were already ahead of the game.

It began with a general feeling of apathy. Actually, I could barely get off the couch to make breakfast for the Ginger Menace. So I ordered *Silver Linings Playbook* on demand, which turned apathy into glassy-eyed immobility, interrupted only by weeping and throwing plastic dishes (me, not my son).

Captain Grief texted while I was packing for my son's sleepover with my sister and brother-in-law. Captain Grief was already excited about her plans for the following day. It was a rare and tender moment when she realized I was not doing so well, so she left obscene messages on my cell phone to cheer me up. What a hero!

That morning, the bright sun had cracked my eyes open early, and then my son's (now thankfully dulled) toes poked up my nose. He had been restless all night in his crib and had flopped through the early morning on the bed next to me. So I slapped myself in the face, we had showers, got dressed, and prepared for our departure to Super Aunt's.

Since the Captain and I were spending the day with our respective groups of friends, we gave one another a running commentary via text:

9:45 a.m.

Me: Sister drove me to yoga. When I hopped out, the Menace looked stunned, but no tears.

CG: Sucker.

Me: [annoyed emoji] Anyways I scored a free class!

CG: Cool. Work up an appetite for the chocolate I got you!

Me: You got me chocolate?

CG: Went to the Eaton Centre, saved an old lady from falling off the escalator!

Me: ?

CG: Bystanders sculpted a life-sized effigy of me with chocolate. You can have my butt.

Me: Uh, no thanks.

CG: My superhero friends said I was showing off. Told them to bite me.

CG: Get it?

Me: Question. Oh where has your elusive chocolate-eating metaphor gone? Answer: Down in flames.

CG: You suck. Where are you?

12:30 p.m.

Me: Brunch with friends. Got a sacrificial plate of French toast and talked about waxing. You?

CG: Riding a camel, not easy. Would be screwed if I wasn't a superhero. [Personal note: I actually rode a camel in Egypt in November 2016 and I think the Captain is just a whiner.] We packed bikinis and went to an oasis.

Me: Can superheroes tan?

CG: Sure! And without the nasty side effects. I didn't take off the mask, it gave me wicked raccoon eyes.

Me: Can't teextttt laaughing toooo hard.

CG: Piss off. And FYI, I just took a poll. None of us wax.

Me: You *are* a superhero!

CG: That, and there is no known force that will yank these follicles out of my skin! Viva la hair!

2:00 p.m.

> Me: At the spa, ready to soak, steam and shiver troubles away.

CG: Shiver?

> Me: Cold plunge. Friends think I'm crazy. I float until I can't feel my extremities, it's very Canadian.

CG: Wow, that's my kind of crazy.

> Me: And so good for inflammation. What you up to?

CG: Can't talk. Surfing a wave of red-hot magma. The board is starting to melt, and so is my…

4:30 p.m.

CG: So this is my new number. The old phone is in a puddle of buttons. Now a hula lesson and a coconut-bra workshop.

> Me: You went to Hawaii?

CG: Nah. Stomping on grapes in Pompeii, reawakened Mount Vesuvius.

> Me: Poor Italians.

CG: Just a little singed. Swearing with your hands really helps express your anger.

> Me: So what's up with hula lessons?

CG: We're at Weebly's House of Slutty Costumes. Party later, we'll be the entertainment.

> Me: That's a safe bet.

8:07 p.m.

>Me: At The Watermark for Irish fare. Is a chicken club with fries Irish?

CG: [Shrug emoji] Eat it with an accent.

>Me: Uh … ta be sure. Where you supping?

CG: Sports bar.

>Me: ???

CG: Only place we can arm wrestle, getting psyched for the The Man of Steel. Lois Lane is hot.

12:00 a.m.

>Me: I'm 35 years old!!

CG: Me too!

>Me: Crews & Tangos is packed.

CG: Meet there!

>Me: No, we're leaving. Some guys groped us. Going to Slack Alice, need lesbos.

CG: What?! There in 10 seconds!

>Me: Don't bother we out. Lesbian Heaven here!

1:15 a.m.

CG: Almost there. Let's close the place down!

>Me: Or head home. Morning comes early … when you distract yourself with an awesome birthday. I pooched.

CG: Okay. Happy Birthday, Kel!

>Me: Happy Birthday, Captain Grief! Xoxox

INTERNATIONAL WIDOWS DAY

Well, you learn something new every day. That's what I said when I learned about International Widows Day, which occurs every year on June 23. And today could be a learning day for you too if you haven't already heard.

This global United Nations observance has been celebrated since 2011. It was created by Raj Loomba of The Loomba Foundation, which was established in 1997. The date for International Widows Day was chosen because the founder's mother became a widow June 23, 1954.

This day was also created in recognition of the hardships that many widows worldwide experience when their partners die. They deal with poverty, serious illness, little or no acknowledgement or care from the government, financial hardship, social injustice, crime, public shame, and everything that sucks.

In some countries, there's even a superstition that widows are bad luck. Sometimes crimes are committed against them and their families (or even by their families). I may not feel lucky to be a widow, but I do feel lucky to be one in Canada. Not only is my marriage valid, like any heterosexual marriage, but I also have access to government assistance and social programming.

When Captain Grief found out about how widows are sometimes treated, she got pretty pissed, so before she destroyed something on behalf of the widows of the world or lit something on fire with the laser beams from her eyes, I told her something important: Anyone can be a superhero and donate to a good cause at www.theloombafoundation.org. Or they can send a widow a card, some chocolates, and a tiara! Life is too short not to wear a tiara!

Captain Grief and I also came up with a list of activities anyone can do to celebrate being a widow…

1. **Get up in the morning with a soundtrack.** With toothbrush, curling iron, or spatula in hand, prance around the house in your pyjamas, singing "I Will Survive."

2. **Do something you've never done before.** It could be as simple as going for a walk in a different neighbourhood, trying a recipe from one of those

magazines on your bookshelf, or enrolling in the Rough and Tumble Rodeo Clown Academy.

3. **Get crafty.** We all have art supplies in our houses, even if only macaroni and glue. Create a noodle collage with glitter, sparkles, and feathers on an old picture frame. Put a photo of your spouse in it and then imagine her/him/them wincing at their new adornments.

4. **Plant something.** Whether it's that tomato plant you wanted, a flat of impatiens, that bouquet of flowers in a vase, or your ass on the couch to watch a movie.

5. **Clean out the [fill in the blank].** Just pick something — the dreaded partner's side of the closet, under the bathroom sink, the garage, or the lint trap in the dryer. In the last case, donate your fluff to a nice mouse house near you. (Widowed mice are easy to spot — they look much more depressed than their squeaky counterparts.)

6. **Invite your pals over for pizza and a pillow fight.** You know you want to. You might braid each other's hair, do facials and pedicures, or haul out the old truth-or-dare routine, depending on how far your friends will go to make this Widows Day a total sparkle fest.

7. **Road trip!** Pack light, get out the map, throw on the Indigo Girls, and get out of town in style.

8. **Make a sign.** One that says "International Widows Day" with a big smiley face, and tape it to your car (or house or the waiter at dinner). Make another sign that says "Widows Rock" and attach it to the other side of the car ... or waiter. Be messy and proud!

Widows of the world, throw on your sequins and unite!
Life is too short to sit out.

POST-PRIDE SLUMP

Ever hear the expression, "Pride goeth before the fall"? Well, in the case of the Toronto Pride celebrations of 2013, they certainly preceded quite a significant drop. That little letdown sensation of the blues must be fairly common in the queer community after a gigantic come-out-of-the-closet party.

It's like a street fair that just came out. It's the place for the dyke who chopped it all off and the drag queen who escaped the house in their mother's heels and cocktail dress. Being visible in your queerness is kind of like a drug in the most after-school-special way. Everyone needs to feel seen, and at Pride you can (a lot).

However, when I lost Kara, my queer family was struck with the same loss of that one beloved and irreplaceable individual. It was wonderful, it was horrible, and then it was wonderful again to be celebrating exciting events away from the pain but also to be up to my eyes in *memory*.

Even though Kara was a social person with great stories, she was not as enamoured of the sparkly shine of Pride as I was. She didn't like crowds and said more than once that if she could manage living on the side of a mountain, she would. Until she remembered how much fun she had with her friends.

I was not alone in a feeling of urgency to congregate, not to mention we had the opportunity to do the Dyke March. I was determined to be nothing if not totally seen and accounted for that first year! Going through some of Kara's keepsakes, I dug out the Italian "Pace" (peace) flag. It gave her a giggle that it was put against the backdrop of the adopted gay symbol, the rainbow. We marched it right down the centre of the road, dancing the whole way, very strategically behind the moving boxing ring full of sparring women. Then the clock struck twelve and the carriages were pumpkins again.

Journal Entry

The Captain and I are currently at the Second Cup sniffing over our Italian sodas, trying to graciously mourn the passing of this holiday. Well the Captain doesn't care so much about being gracious. While I'm sniffing over my journal, she's curled up in the fetal position under the table, gumming a Pride flag. I think it's fair to say she's down for the count this week.

I would laugh, except for the fact that *I get it*. I needed to come here and witness the bedraggled rainbow decorations flapping weakly in the wind in order to really believe it was over. It was a great vacation from grief to lose myself in the rainbow effect, but being back in the bosom of queerness is a whole lot less bosomy than it was last weekend.

I've passed other Prides with much less depression, but this year, avoiding the reality of my sudden single-mom status (Super Mom volunteered to babysit), it occurred to me that I really needed and enjoyed a break from a pretty harsh reality. Being alone in the house after the Ginger Menace is in bed is not pleasant. Sometimes it can be quite torturous.

You can't hide from grief when there's no one else around, but Pride sure fixed that. Pride is gay Christmas!

And now I'm like a kid after gay Christmas, watching a naked, slightly tinselled tree lying on the curb. I guess Pride does bear a lot of similarities to my other favourite holiday. At Christmas, I'm guaranteed the comfort of family and food, social interaction, physical affection, and childcare — all things that a single mother desperately needs when the holiday hits, especially after the November anniversaries of the deaths of a parent and a spouse.

Just like at Christmas, the stress of loss triggers a lot of emotion, particularly for a bereaved person. I find I get terrified over even small losses, and really any change is a loss. So this year at Pride I went full tilt to escape. Butch Femme Salon on Thursday, Queer Movie Friday, and the Dyke March and dancing in my bikini at the beer garden on Saturday. Then I promptly collapsed in a glorious heap of tears on Saturday night before pulling myself together to wrap things up with a barbecue!

Now, as many of my friends work their way through Pride Recovery Week, I'm left wondering, How do I help them? And how do I help myself crawl out of the pit of despair? Well, I guess the same way I always do. I write a list.

Behind me, as if on command, Captain Grief stirs, and she's ready to write (well mostly nod), having blown her nose on a stray napkin and climbed into the chair. Here we go:

Ten ways to alleviate a post-Pride slump...

1. Go down to The Village. It'll remind you that The Village is still there, give you some closure, and help you process the loss of Pride Week.

2. Have your friends over. *Pride is where your pals are!* Then roleplay funny or embarrassing moments from this and maybe next year's Pride.

3. Watch a hilarious gay movie. I recommend To Wong Foo, Thanks for Everything! Julie Newmar; Connie and Carla; But I'm a Cheerleader; Victor/Victoria; or Imagine Me and You. If you want something a little longer, try a marathon of The L Word or Queer as Folk.

4. Get some exercise; go to a mall entrance or some other building with a revolving door. Run in a circle repeatedly and every time you pass your exit yell, "I'm out of the closet!"

5. Sing or cry, as appropriate, to gay or lesbian artists. Melissa Etheridge, Ani DiFranco, Indigo Girls, George Michael, or Elton John.

6. Read some good gay books. Sarah Waters's *Tipping the Velvet* is beautiful. I also love Jeanette Winterson's *Oranges Are Not the Only Fruit* and, of course, *Lost Boi* by Sassafras Lowrey (steamy), or anything by Ivan Coyote.

7. Frequent the monthly Toronto or Montreal Queer Slowdance. (This Saturday is a beach-blanket theme. It'll be like a reunion!)

8. Sneak around the city in wings with a jar of sparkles, offering light gay dustings.

9. Learn a new gay fact. Feel proud as a peacock? When I was watching cartoons, I learned that a group of peacocks is called a party. A party of peacocks? Sounds queer to me!

10. Cuddle up with something comforting and gay. For me it's the gayest bed linens that ever gayed: a rainbow plastered with two Sandra Boynton cats saying, "Keep smiling." Mom got these for me before I came out. I love proud, psychic parents!

CHAPTER FIVE
"I GOT THE POWER!"

"Are you shitting me?" The Captain blinked through the haze of the London Fog sitting in front of her.

"Whatever are you talking about?" I decided to play dumb — and also fully enjoy an opportunity to outdo her in a number of dramatic ways.

Captain Grief looked around nervously, hoping no one was staring. She was wrong. She looked back at me, eyes still bugging at my apparel. "Um, I think the rainbow tube top, tiara, and sparkly pink-flamingo pants are a tad dressed up for a normal day on Danforth Avenue. You look like a float."

I had big news to share, and I kind of wanted to test her commitment to staying put, even before I dropped the bomb. Hence the flamboyant outfit. "Cool, that suits a queer-positive ice cream shop."

"Funny." She crossed her arms in disapproval and started tapping her boot on the floor.

"Thanks, I thought so." I didn't really know how this conversation was going to go. *She assumes she has one up on me*, I thought, *just because she can hogtie villains, like the Smelly Colossus, and jump buildings in a single bound. Well I think we're on par when it comes to wit and the public use of gallows humour. I guess Captain Grief figures the resemblance stops right there.*

"Friggin' hell, you're irritatingly perky today. Would you at least take off the boa?" she said, swatting a pink feather that almost landed in her cup. "Everybody's looking."

I smirked, considering her absolute obliviousness to the fact that a banana-yellow cape, yellow leather boots, a blue mask, and spandex jumpsuit were a tad atypical for East Toronto as well. *Oh, this is fun*, I thought. "No, no one's looking. Well, except for that butch in the corner." I pointed and waved. The Captain flinched and hid behind her cup. "I think I may have induced a femme mating ritual."

"Holy crap, you're embarrassing. Just say what you have to say so I can go home."

"Want me to get under the table?"

"Bite me."

"It would be easier that way."

"For fuck sake, would you get to the point?"

I sighed with a little trepidation, but it had to be done. I had to come out of the superhero closet. "Sure, sorry. I needed you here, so possibly you would make less of a scene."

"You're firing me?" The pregnant pause bounced around the room, and I could see lava starting to boil behind her eyes. She stood up to leave.

"No, no, I just meant that you might not want to hurt innocent bystanders." I grabbed her cape and hoped she wouldn't keep walking.

She looked over her shoulder at me. "Why?"

"Well, I want to break it to you gently, but I've been hiding a secret."

She turned, doing a one-eighty in mood and stance. "You're moving to Switzerland." She put her hands together in prayer. "Please say you're moving to Switzerland."

"Nice try, but no. I wanted to tell you that … I have a superpower."

She was genuinely taken aback for a moment, but then her expression changed as I watched her assume this was a part of a joke, just like my pants. She smiled, resumed her seat, and took a sip of tea. Then she laughed.

"Well, unless you can play leapfrog on the sun and not come home with a scorched ass, then I think I have you beat."

"No, no, it's nothing as spectacular as that."

"Go on, Fluffy."

"Well … I've just started to develop this—"

"Rash! Yes, an itchy, oozy one!"

"Put a lid on it, Air Miles" I looked at her disgruntled and put down my cup. "So I've discovered I have this ability to … move forwards in time."

"Come again?"

I smiled at her bemused look and soaked in the moment before the plunge. "I can time travel."

"Wait, for one flying second…"

I could see her trying to do some sort of calculation to disprove my claim, but then slow realization crept across her features, and she looked at me like she had never seen me before. "We're joined at the hip. How did I not notice this?"

"Well, you've had a lot on your mind, and it's way less impressive than a fireproof butt."

"I'll say! Are you using your power for good or evil? If it's the latter, I have the number of a great twenty-step program."

"I'll let you know if I develop a time travel addiction. Point is, I wanted to do a demonstration."

"In a public place?" She indicated the shop and the patrons eating gelato and cake. "If going forwards in time will cause the current timeline to disappear in a 'Flashy' blue inferno I say, hell no."

"Don't you want to know a bit about our future … just one teeny year?"

She leaned in, trying not to look curious. She failed. "Go on."

"It's just, this Year of Firsts is so hard. So I wanted to see how things would change for us. I jumped forward one year. To Pride 2014. That will actually be when World Pride is held right here in Toronto."

"Are you shitting me?" Her mouth split into the kid-at-gay-Christmas gasp and she gripped the table, jiggling the cups.

"Not in the least." I mopped up the spilled tea and smiled, knowing I had her. "First off, you look fabulous-er. And I've come out of the performance closet."

"Okay, bye."

I grabbed her arm. "Sit your cool ass down. What I mean is, I haven't been on a stage in years, and I certainly haven't read my work in public for a very long time. Well, 2014 is the year that will change."

"Holy hot buns, Mr. Bakerman."

"Yeah, it really was, er, will be an amazing year." I counted the glorious events of 2014 on my fingers as I listed them. "World Pride, Melissa Etheridge in town (and I get to write a feature article in *Pink Play*!), two of my close friends will get hitched at a mass wedding at Casa Loma, and I'll be selected for a Nuit Rose event. I get to stand up on stage and read a memoir piece called, 'My Butch Wife.'"

"I've got to see this." She grabbed my arm like I'd just asked her to race trains down to Union with me. I took a brown bag from my purse and handed it to her.

"I don't think you can doggy bag ice cream, genius."

"Just take the bag. Time travel can be a little hard on the digestive tract at first."

"Evil." She scowled.

I smiled … a little. "Wait till I take you to 2016. It'll blow your effing mind. But for now, hang on…"

I closed my eyes, tapped my pink-sequined kitten heels three times, and the shop started to shake. The customers around us didn't seem to notice. In the monstrous wind that was starting up, I shouted, "These are actually just normal shoes! But they make time travel look way more flashy!"

I hate you, she mouthed as her cape flew up over her head and she was lifted from her seat. The scene around us flickered like celluloid in a projector. I grabbed the Captain's suit. She raised the bag to her mouth and tossed her cookies, as we moved forwards in time.

MY BUTCH WIFE

She was so butch. Her pockets were always filled with coins for the parking meter, Swiss Army knives, and that tube of cherry-flavoured lip chap. I remember watching her put it on one day, drawing it across her lips like it was a marker or like she was greasing a hinge. Perfunctory, expedient, not like she was enjoying the colour or how sexy it made her lips feel. I remember thinking, *You couldn't apply lipstick if your life depended on it*. Well, she could, but it would just look very … well, gay, if it has to be said. Kara was Kara. She was my butch wife, her love for that Winnie-the-Pooh dress at seven years old notwithstanding … that was the way she was. So no one was surprised when she came out.

A few days before our wedding, I went and got a mani-pedi with my bridesmaids, and over a glass of wine, I told them the story of the time Kara went for a pedicure. About how she practically had to arm wrestle the hot-pink nail polish out of the small esthetician's hands and convince her to give her only a clear coat "if she had to."

I love how, by just being herself, my wife changed others. Changed their perspective, their outlook, their understanding. She didn't mean to be a walking billboard for gay rights and gender expression, she just "came out" that way. When my Uncle Bob met her at an art show, the first thing she did was give him a sturdy handshake, hoist a load of his daughter's display shelving onto her shoulder, and walk it to his car. I think he was in love, or at least very impressed. No, he was absolutely in love.

He phoned my mother right away and said, "Gayle! Have you met her?"

"No."

"Well," Bob continued, "you're going to love her."

When I took her to their house for the annual cousins Christmas party, Aunt Susan gave her a loot bag full of nail files and girly sticky notes in a makeup case. She just smiled and passed it to me in the car after we left. And I love how the day after, Bob approached my mother at breakfast to clarify something.

"So, when Kara comes to Barb's wedding she'll be wearing … a suit?" So tentative, so careful, so accepting. And Aunt Susan learned to modify her holiday gift bag. She grew to understand Kara, which always seemed to lead to loving her.

"Half girl stuff, half boy stuff," Kara said, smiling, when we got in the car after the next year's party. "Good enough, she gets it."

With those who did *not* get it, I tried my best to be patient, as long as they were respectful. With those who could not get past her exterior, I often thought, *What's there to get? She's a chick who dresses like a man.* There was nothing, at least outwardly, that equated her with the prototypical idea of feminine — other than the fact that she was a stunning woman. To me, just her existence made things evident. The way she wore that "this is me" attitude, she ended up changing the people around her, challenging them to take her exactly as she was. Whether they were up for the challenge was totally up to them.

I also saw, over and over, how we were "that couple" to so many people. The safe, oddly familiar, yet indisputably different pair. The dry run. We were the training wheels to a whole bevy of people who had never heard of gender-neutral pronouns, packing, or bathroom harassment. Most times they had never even thought of it. We were the couple people timidly approached to ask personal questions, to which Kara would habitually respond, "Well, if you have the balls to ask, I have the balls to answer!" She was a statement and the statement said, "Deal with it."

She also extended herself to others gently, and gathered folks in. Everything about her said stay a while, come into my kitchen, hear a story, be comforted, try the food, share my memories, and learn to understand the world better. Sometimes I would have this inconclusive feeling, as I tried to catalogue her traits with regards to gender association, but it was that mix that held the mystery and made me conclude, That's the woman I love.

There's also a part of my brain that remembers with horror and shame the "It's Pat" sketch on *Saturday Night Live*. The sketch I watched and laughed at. The overexaggerated, grotesque character who was neither man nor woman, and therefore savagely mocked, was so removed from reality or from my reality at the time. It pains me to think of the scores of intersex, transgender, transcurious, or gender fluid youths who saw that and were a little more afraid.

Kara knew that sharp, judgmental gaze, and she got used to it. So much so that it never seemed to more than graze her skin, even if it stuck into her heart. She would jokingly refer to it as the "what-is-it look," and most times I feel like I was angrier about it than she was. I remember going to a Coleman warehouse sale to get cheap camping gear in what she called Hetero-sauga (Mississauga). Hand in hand, we walked along the long, long, long line of ambivalent-to-horrified onlookers, and we must have received the what-is-it look a hundred times. She was tense, and I was livid but glad to glare back.

Even though I knew at the age of nineteen that women who looked like men turned my crank, I did not, at that time, equate that with my life, the choices I would make, the worlds I would visit, and the love I would share. How humbled, how grateful I feel that the Universe presented me with such a gift. A person to share my life with. A wife and a husband. A mother and a father for my child. A soft place, a strong voice, an easy laugh, an ironclad loyalty, and a carefree manner, whose place in my world is now empty.

Journal Entry

I have to count how many months it's been to be sure. How much time has passed since she died. Seven months. We were together for seven years, and now I'm sitting here, drinking a beer and remembering. In the holistic healing circles that I'm a part of, they say that seven years is a transformative cycle. *Transformative*. It's such a powerful, uplifting word for a concept that involves so much pain.

I think about it when I'm washing bottles and folding laundry. At the same time as thinking about what an irreplaceable person she was, I'm also wondering what the hell I'm going to do with all those novelty t-shirts? At the same time as wondering how anyone else could ever make me that happy, I'm dreading sorting out the workshop, mowing the lawn, and raising our son alone. It feels like it doesn't matter what questions I ask, because right now I don't have the answers.

FLOOD OF GRIEF

Just when I thought it had all happened in 2013, the worst flood on record since 1954 hit Toronto. I know I wasn't the only one feeling up the creek without a paddle, but at least I didn't have to canoe home. I learned about it watching television at my place after a vacation with Super Mom.

On the last day at my mother's, the Ginger Menace had woken up gasping for breath and I had forgotten his puffer. There's nothing like a wheezing child to send me into abject fear. I remember when my son first exhibited signs of breathing issues. He woke up croupy, and when steam and lavender did no good, we called our moms and Telehealth Ontario, who all said the same thing: Take him into the cold. It helps. And we said, what? I remember watching through the kitchen window as Kara bounced him around in his snowsuit, praying it would help.

When we got to the hospital, his breathing had indeed eased up, but they put him in an adult-sized hospital gown (the only one on hand) and an oxygen mask. He looked so small and my heart bled watching him. I gained such an appreciation that night for the fears that a parent must somehow conquer in order to cope. The doctor sent us home with a puffer and an AeroChamber to administer it with (and what fun that was!).

Well that morning at Mom's, there was no puffer, and I was unceremoniously ushered into the guilt of the first emerg visit without my wife. Even though Mom was there, so was the same spine-tingling fear. I could barely control my swirl of emotions to collect our belongings and get into the car to drive to the hospital — terror at being alone, doubt about whether I could really do this on my own, anger at myself, anger at Kara for not being there, and a desperately deep feeling of her absence.

As I waited for the doctor, I amused myself by looking at the medical supplies, because what else is there to do when you're waiting for a doctor? The Ginger Menace wanted to know what everything was, and as I perused the cart in front of me, my eyes were drawn to what looked like a thermos, except there was a label on it that read "Human eyes"!

I couldn't help but snort and let the sarcasm roll in. *Really? Is that something you should leave lying around in a waiting room?* Then I thought, *Well, I guess every specimen needs an appropriate receptacle*, and finally, I couldn't help it, *Well it's nice to know my wife is looking out for me, with the exact same sense of humour!*

Back in Toronto, the biting irony of the flood we faced was that I had finally gotten back into a kayak that weekend for the first time since summer camp, and had felt *much more confident on the water*. Eye roll. But when I turned on the news that evening I didn't feel so confident. I would have called Captain Grief, but she was in India sitting on the Taj Mahal, meditating on her anger issues.

The waters continued to rise, and I tried to channel Kara and her coolheadedness as I rounded up candles, lighters, and flashlights, stored water in the fridge, made up some bottles, and charged my phone, but this preparation was not enough to make me feel at ease. I needed the emergency backpack.

If we'd ever had the occasion to lash together a raft and paddle down the Don River, you can bet Kara would have been the one wearing the emergency backpack because it weighed a bloody ton. My wife was military grade for preparedness — she picked up emergency supplies for fun. She was a powerhouse mix: wilderness survivor; cadet-trained, militia-flavoured medic; security guard; volunteer firefighter/paramedic; and Northern Ontario bouncer. That backpack was a perfect metaphor for the role she played for family and friends. She would try to carry everything on her shoulders, even when it weighed her down.

She would push through a crowd at a club, with me in tow, and the drunk lesbians and gay boys would part like water. She was completely sanguine in the knowledge that she could not be intimidated. So much so that she was amused by the challenge.

"Go ahead," she would say when someone unwisely threatened her. "Try it. It'll be *funny*."

This was what I was used to having. Used to counting on. This is why, with the sinking realization that she was not there to stand between us and any possible emergency situation, I was catapulted into *the sheer panic of another unexpected but inevitable first.*

As I went through her backpack, I knew I could lighten the load. Her work gloves, masks, rubber booties, and (after a short conversation with her) the machete had to go. Also, I couldn't see myself making room for the hazmat suits, the ten cans of tuna, or the portable stove.

Yet it still made me sick to think that the Ginger Menace and I could be alone and possibly need something I'd removed.

Everyone worries, and I think having a child kicks that into high gear. I had to be prepared, as it was the only way I would have the courage to turn off the news and go to bed. After disemboweling a number of Kara's first aid kits, including her medic bag from cadets, I sat on the couch in a nest of self-adhesive and tensor bandages, iodine pads, and neatly rolled gauze, and went into shock. It was too much. Just the process of elimination was agony. I could never expect to do what she did. Then I had a good old cry and realized that was the point. *I am not supposed to be her. I am just supposed to remember her.*

Journal Entry

I spun my wheels until about two a.m., until my eyes stung and I couldn't even see what I was packing anymore. When I woke up in the morning to my toddler pulling my arm, trying to haul himself up to the bed, I realized, *This is stupid*. I knew it was stupid last night, but I couldn't stop myself.

Now, in the cold light of eight o'clock (thank God it isn't six), I know I took my expectations to a completely fanatical place. This was confirmed when I tried to pick up the backpack. It still felt like a bag of rocks, even without the damn machete. But I am trying to love my mistakes because they are a part of the same process that gets you to fewer bad mistakes, to neutral decisions, and then to success.

Perhaps it was trying to pick up my toddler right after the backpack that clinched it. What am I going to do? Crawl on all fours hauling a backpack that feels like it's full of dumbbells? Strap a diaper bag to my side and pull the Ginger Menace on a sled with my teeth? After emergency-prep panic and fatigue-induced hysteria, I decided, yes. Apparently, that *is* the plan.

Just like all the decisions in my life that have come out of suddenly being a single mom, I know that again *I can't expect myself to do things the way she did, if it doesn't work for me.* I could never keep up with that. I wouldn't be happy. It has to do with ownership of my life. Reclaiming the things I have, acknowledging my strengths, and being the support I need for myself.

So I'll pack diapers, bottles, a first aid kit, meds, snacks, water, flashlight, emergency blanket, sunscreen, hats, matches, iodine, light toiletries, a map, emergency numbers, socks, change, light entertainment, whistles, a pocket knife, lavender essential oil, Rescue Remedy (an herbal essence blend for shock), and a journal (writing keeps me sane!).

I'll also pack my stories. They're weightless and won't be going anywhere. I'll pack my endurance, since I'm gonna need it. I also hope to make room for optimism and a sense of humour. The only thing I'm still on the fence about is the machete. I may want to hang on to that one as a keepsake.

UNDER MY SKIN

Grief is big. I think perhaps that's why it's so intimidating for people who haven't had a lot of experience with it. I've spoken about the social awkwardness of grief many times. It feels like crashing a party by pulling up in a big red flame-engulfed covered wagon. People don't know whether to stand and gawk, feed the fire, or run for the garden hose.

There's another part to grief that can be even worse than tearing up in the supermarket in front of strangers. It's the part that doesn't come out at parties. It's the deep, dark well. It's the part that howls at night. The part of you that stands stock-still on the street corner in the utter confoundedness of how "this" could have happened.

That's the function of shock. Not many people can process that kind of trauma right away, so after the numbing immobilization subsides, delayed grief commences. To those who can compartmentalize, it may be on the shelf, but it's not going anywhere. When you actually let yourself feel the emotions that accompany it, it takes time to again notice your feet on the ground and climb back into your body. I'm past that stage, but that doesn't mean I don't visit it. Sometimes the well and I have a good long catch-up. During that first year, it would sometimes sleep on my couch for weeks at a time. It was like a (very deep) wading pool in my living room, and I had to lift the bottoms of my pyjama pants in the morning to cross it on the way to the kitchen.

Journal Entry

The loss of my partner confounds me, and now living life without her confounds me even more. I've been working my way around how to make some necessary decisions in my life, and have found I can't avoid the pool. You'd think I would be grateful for a pool in my living room with how hot it is this week. Every time I trip over it and fall in, I cry like a baby and end up even more hot, sticky, and snotty than before.

Sure, I miss my wife, but the part that's really getting to me is how my life is going to change now that she's not here. I am afraid, I am overwhelmed, and I am terrified to willingly create more change in my life. Of course, much good can come from change, but that does nothing to lessen the fear of moving on and the guilt of moving away from the life I once had.

It's another loss when you realize you're strong enough and brave enough to stand on your own.

It really is the little miracles, like a small crisis, that knock you down and give you the chance to overcome.

I don't know when or where the glass got broken, but one night I noticed that a piece of glass was lodged in the middle of my foot. It's not that I couldn't deal with it on my own; it was just awkward as ass without some help. I turned on the light, pulled out the tweezers, and managed to dig it out. Crisis averted. If you're wondering what the next challenge was, it was the same, except it was a splinter, and not in my foot but my hand. Simple, right? Wrong. It was in my right hand. *How the frig will I deal with this?*

Once more, I dug out my tweezers. It was even more awkward. I waved my left hand around in spastic attempts at dexterity, and all of a sudden, the tips of the tweezers chomped down on that nasty wooden interloper. I don't think I've ever been so excited to desplinter myself. And I bet you're wondering, did it end there?

It didn't.

My sister-in-law, my nieces, the Ginger Menace, and I were at the car races at Mosport. The kids looked so cute in their protective head gear. They had blue tongues from the popsicles, they had their pictures taken in a race car, and they climbed all over the wooden bleachers. It was a late night, and I didn't realize until bath time the following evening that there was another splinter, but in my son's hand this time.

After the production that nail trimming required, I was shaking in my sweaty tank top. How was I going to do this? I put him on my lap and went in with the tweezers. He freaked out. So, like a surprised cop at a hold-up, I put down my weapon and reasoned with him. *I villainized the splinter.*

"Look, look." I pointed it out to him like it was news. "Look at that bad, bad splinter! What's it doing in there? That doesn't belong there! Let's see if Mommy can get it!" I pulled at it. It was definitely a splinter. I picked away at the thin layer of skin over the top of it. The Ginger Menace was thankfully engrossed. Slowly, I began to see more of the splinter and made a few quick swipes for it. Drum roll ... and it was out. I did an internal dance.

I think these miracles are akin to training wheels. It is okay to celebrate small. It is okay to build on success and do things slowly. One day it may be a splinter in your toddler's hand, and the next day it might be finding a job. I just have to remind myself that I will fall in the pool sometimes, that *I am* the splash zone — so don't stand too close because you'll get soaked. But I *can* save myself, even if I save myself one way or one story at a time.

And speaking of the splash zone, Captain Grief was very leery after our last time-travel episode, so she disrespectfully declined my invitation to jump ahead again, even just a few months. She said she had her hero work to continue (but I saw her skipping rocks over her pool again, aware that she's avoiding her grief). And also, I think she's afraid to get sucked down a wormhole and end up butt-naked in her sixth-grade French class. I hear superhero schools are hell.

Journal Entry

The interlocking stone path under the wheels of the stroller remained unchanged, but when I put my foot on the supposed solid ground, it squelched and squirmed. I felt the urge to cry, but the recent, overly zealous rain seemed to make my tears redundant.

It rained the day before and all through the night. I slept with the window open and let the cool wind tumble relief all over my clammy, summer-evening skin. Now the slowly warming day had begun and I was out of excuses.

Anticipation of pain is in many ways worse than the pain itself, but now it was Tuesday, and it was time. I had cash. I had time off. I was returning to the market.

Shrines are not just walls of pictures and collections of keepsakes. They are also songs, activities, places, and times of the year. The grounds of the East York Civic Centre was one of those immovable shrines. It had been a small frozen labyrinth all winter. The snowy stone paths, strewn with empty, frosted flower beds and large sections of crunchy grass were a natural shortcut to our house, but at a cost. Cutting through this expanse inevitably led to showers of tears, which made me nickname the place "bawl-your-face-off park." It was as if I could still see the ghost of the seasonal farmers' market that we had frequented as a family as often as we could. Walking through it anytime since last November, I couldn't help but remember the square of tables in the main section, covered in little green baskets filled with colourful produce. I could see long white canopies sheltering the farmers and the people buying fruits and vegetables. And somewhere swirling in among the same frozen recollection, she was there: the ghost of my wife.

The skies were suddenly blue again on that day in 2013, but I only registered what felt like a temporary relief. I went straight to the couple selling mushrooms on the corner, and took another breath. I had wondered on many occasions if they would remember me, if they would remember us, when we were all of us. Last year when we still had Kara, my son and I used to be there every week and had chatted to them about vacation plans. Once, when I didn't have enough money for my usual bag of cremini mushrooms, the gentleman flashed me a smile and said, "Pay me next week." He was astounded when I returned with a toonie, and expounded for a good couple of minutes on the virtue of honesty and the nature of good folk.

This time around, he just asked me what I would like. He smiled the same gentle smile and handed me a brown paper bag while teasing my son and making him giggle.

I felt like a statue trying to form a smile out of the unrelenting material I had to work with. No, it wasn't a smile: It was just that the shape of my mouth changed a little and it passed for a smile. I looked at him and wondered, *Do you know that I'm dead inside? Can you tell that I am, at this moment, a walking, talking shadow?*

He did not. No one did. It is the profoundness of the pain of grieving that makes the griever think it must be visible.

I turned and continued down the line to the other vendors, but I had to stop myself and go in the opposite direction, along the route we usually walked. Hitting the large vegetable booth closest to the northwest entrance of the market, a sense of familiarity set in. Anything else would have been strange and unnecessarily painful.

And so our summer market visits began again with small multicoloured tomatoes, a basket of mini cucumbers, tender zucchini, and two bunches of slender asparagus. *Breathing easier now*, I thought, as I tied the bag to the stroller and headed to the honey booth. I'd been craving honey on toast for a few days and being able to fulfill this ripe desire now was satisfying.

I saw the jars of bee pollen and smiled, at least internally, to remember how the vendors had almost convinced me to take this popular delicacy home to my wife. There was a theory going around in the holistic community that taking a small dose of bee pollen would "cure" seasonal allergies. Kara suffered the constant inconveniences and indignities of all-season allergies.

As I told her about this new and wonderful product, I had only to look at her face to know she thought the theory was total bunk. Kara was an open-minded person with a holistic practitioner for a wife, but her expression made me realize that a jar of bee pollen was the last thing I should ever bring home from a market. It's a good thing I settled on a jar of creamed honey instead.

At the next stall, I saw the little purple vegetables that had made me reevaluate my estimation of eggplant as a mushy, stringy substance. Kara and I started off with the small "adorable-sized" eggplants, this size being my invented catchphrase, in reference to my mother and her love of all things baby-sized. As soon as we were hooked, we moved on to the grown-up size. We cut the large wheels of eggplant and massaged them in a mix of olive oil, fresh dill, and lemon. These were the kind of vegetables that stood up to the grill.

And with a barbecue just outside the back door (instead of up a flight of stairs, like at our old apartment) it made patio dining easy. Plus, we were consuming the kind of summer-fresh fare that made us want to eat dinner on the back deck every night: long dill-speckled strips of zucchini, large plump mushrooms, and round spiral-patterned onions.

It was no wonder we ended up having so many barbecues for our friends. I lost count of the number of times Kara went for propane. It was these outdoor celebrations that made me feel no loss for the little third-floor patio we left behind. This was permanent; this was what made it feel like home.

I had to draw a breath looking at the kids running in the square around the market, at the white canopies, the babies with messy faces snuggled to their parents, the dogs on leashes hunting down the prevalent smell of bread and beef in the air, the nurses and doctors in scrubs buying food on their break. The slow, gentle gait of everyone around made them seem unperturbed by any kind of existential crisis.

I went for cheese. The youngish curly-headed, bearded man slivered off a sample from a number of white wedges and passed them to me delicately from the tip of his knife. Ben chomped down on the goat-milk Camembert, and I smiled widely, remembering how Kara felt about goat cheese.

"It tastes like dirty socks."

My response was obvious in the "How do you know you don't like it, if you haven't tried dirty socks?" way, but she never gave me an answer. I bought a hard goat cheese and tucked it into the cool well of produce, in the bag we had not yet filled. It was only ten thirty or so, and when I got to the barbecue grilling station, I thought, *It's too early to justify a hot dog.* Even if the memory of Kara's preferred lunch, a hot dog covered in mustard and sauerkraut, was luring me in.

At that moment, I became aware of a conversation. Near me, a child said to her mother, "I can see the hospital."

"Yes," she answered. "It's the building with the big blue H."

Yes, I said in my mind. Yes, I can't forget that just a block down the street was where my wife died, twice, before they got her into the ambulance to go to another hospital. I feel like she waited for me, waited until I had seen her through the glass, and maybe she could see me too.

She was unconscious, but I feel sure she knew I was there. In the waiting room, I also knew in the pit of my stomach that when the alarms went off and staff went pelting back down that hall, it was because she was trying to escape from her body. This is not something you forget, especially when you're with your son at a farmers' market just up the street from that place where it all happened.

I almost didn't register the change at the grilling stall, but then I caught the scent of fresh bread in the air. The bakery truck was now parked here, rather than in its usual spot at the north entrance. The long, slender loaves they sold, called pizza sticks, beckoned to my heart through my nose, the baked cheese and the familiar tangy spice catching it. These were the treats we got most weeks.

Five or six to a bag, all still stuck together from baking in the same pan, I made a grab for them and they almost collapsed under the pressure of my grasp. Breaking one apart for the two of us, the bright flavour of the tomato hit the back of my palate, and for a moment I was made motionless by memory. For a minute, Kara was there, not because anything had changed, but because she was indistinguishable from the moment.

After buying a quart of the first local strawberries, I got a hot dog anyway; the market was too small, the errand too quick. I sat on a bench and tried to tempt Ben with my hot dog. He always liked Kara's better. He was having no more of the stroller, so I agreed to let him out after I bought a yellow cherry tomato plant, and we headed home.

Later that day, winding through the park a second time, on our way home from the last swimming class of the season, I looked at the grounds, the wide divots in the earth that the market stalls and people's feet had made. It was empty again, but this time around, it did not feel as haunted. As if this single pilgrimage had put some uneasy spirit of the past to rest. It said, *You need to fill me with the future, with the present, with the now, because I cannot be "was" and "used to" forever.*

CAPTAIN POUTY-PANTS UNINVITES ME TO A PARTY

Near the end of that summer, I noticed that it had been a rough week. And while it was, it also occurred to me that every week was rough — I was grieving, after all. In the same way, every week was also a host to many delights and joys. I didn't have to dwell on the negative stuff if I didn't want to. I could justifiably say that week was business as usual. Well, other than the fact that Captain Grief's mom made her invite me to the Family Superhero picnic, and I felt like I was back in grade school.

She told me confidentially, as she passed me some corn on the cob, that her daughter really had been sulking for long enough about my new superpower and it was time to let it go. It was her longest stand yet — the Captain really doesn't like being upstaged. This dislike was almost a nemesis, like streak-free glass doors!

Yeah, that was messy. I told her mom that my shiny shoes and I would just hang out for a bit, and then get going. But then I overheard part of a fascinating conversation, and since the Ginger Menace was using one of the supersiblings as a Jet Ski in the pool, I figured I might as well get comfortable and listen to the rest.

As I heard the Captain carrying on, it occurred to me that because my friends had been helping me out, she was probably not aware of some other issues I deal with. Sure, you might have guessed that I'm a lesbian, and the fact that I'm a widow might not have escaped you… and perhaps, you also might have heard that I'm a single mom. But there's something else that affects me every day that you don't know about.

I have fibromyalgia. And that week I had a flare-up with a 102-degree fever. I'd been diagnosed with the chronic pain condition when I was twelve. Back in 1990, fibromyalgia was generally scoffed at and given such attractive pseudonyms as "the yuppie flu." Because they couldn't explain it or get conclusive results while investigating it, the medical approach was that it didn't exist and it was to be treated as a psychological condition rather than a physiological one.

Back when I was diagnosed and getting to know the new me (with fibro), I learned how to pull myself out of a slump and find my internal survivor. I joined a choir, got involved in theatre, and sang in my first musical, *Nunsense*, as Sister Robert Anne, affectionately described by peers as the questionably virtuous nun from Brooklyn and the comic relief. It amuses me to think of the witch hat and the Carmen Miranda hat I got to wear over my habit for different numbers.

For the first time, I got to explore my funny! How things stay the same, eh? Add a cape, mask, and boots, put it in an angry blender on high for fourteen seconds, and you basically get Captain Grief.

When it came to dusting myself off after a massive life change, this was my first super incarnation. I also reinvested my energy into my creative writing. However, the comedic writing — well, I just did that as a joke. Comedy was never serious for me, so I never took it seriously.

I was a poet. I wrote memoir and fiction and short stories. Stephanie Fahey (the first brilliant illustrator of Captain Grief) and I could often be seen in the library, she with her drawings of Ziggy, and I with my high school rewrite of *The Terrible, Horrible, No Good, Very Bad Day*.

I think I also made lists, and I vividly remember drawing my own caped crusader for that time in my life, Captain Fibromyalgia, on a lined three-holed piece of scrap paper. She had the cape, the mask, the boots, and most likely the unapologetic attitude. In fact, she and Captain Grief are cousins, and I had no idea until I met her at the picnic.

Once I had picked the corn out of my teeth, I took a deep breath and went over to introduce myself. Captain Fibro was gesturing wildly and telling what must have been a harrowing tale, much to Captain Grief's total amusement. So much so that she didn't see me approach.

And then I said, "Who the hell do you think I am, Hancock?"

Captain Fibro stopped, stood at attention, and made a salute, which Captain Grief mimicked. Then Captain Fibro shouted, "Pause to offer a superhero salute to the eventually unimpeachable Will Smith and his dazzling, powerful superhero wife Charlize Theron in this, one of our favourite superhero flicks. We adore you!"

I couldn't help myself at that point. "Hell yeah." I smiled and joined them.

In *Hancock*, Charlize Theron plays a superhero/goddess-turned-mom-in-hiding who is found out by her male counterpart and forthwith kicks his ass. This shared movie love seemed to break the ice between us picnickers. Her cousin looked at me with interest, but only smiled, while Captain Grief crossed her arms.

"Anyway," said Captain Fibro. "Medical-grade marijuana or not, that stuff will do jack shit for my super condition!"

Captain Grief snorted.

I took that moment to interject, "Excuse me, Captain Fibromyalgia, I think we've met before." She turned to me with confusion, but then she did a double take, and must have seen what I saw.

"No, no, no!" Captain Grief threw her arms up and started toward me. "Not the time turner."

"Wait, Cuz, she's right! Hey, she's the one you're writing the book with!"

"Yeah, she's the writer; I'm the awesome."

I was going to say something snarky, but figured that may be dangerous to my person. Then Captain Fibro shushed her cousin and asked, "So where did we meet?"

"Uh, I think we went to school together." I moved away from Captain Grief who seemed to be emitting some sort of static electricity as her hair was starting to stand on end. "I guess you don't recognize me without the tie and kilt."

"Holy crap, yeah! How are you?" Captain Grief's wattage seemed to be increasing, so her cousin turned to her and said, "Oh, stick it in a socket!" She turned back to me. "She's just mad because you made her lose her lunch." Captain Grief huffed and sat down in a lawn chair.

Captain Fibro continued, "I was telling Captain Grief about the latest dipshit that looked sideways at me for using an accessibility elevator. I may look like a superhero, but that doesn't mean I have all the same powers! Sure, I'm disabled, but I don't need to sit in a wheelchair just so you can tell!"

"You know it." I nodded, thinking about how I sometimes felt when riding the elevator with other folks using canes, walkers, and wheelchairs; that is, like I had to justify something.

"You too?" She pointed at me. "Wait, have we had this conversation before?"

"Probably. I tend to attract people who understand chronic pain and its inconveniences."

She nodded heartily and, out of the corner of my eye, I noticed Captain Grief sit up and listen. Most likely asking herself if there was another thing that she, my superhero alter ego, had failed to notice during her orbit around planet Me. More than likely.

I continued a little louder. "Who cares if I have to duck out on social events at the last minute, need more rest stops, food stops, and 'stop looking at me like that' stops?"

"Yes!!!" Captain Fibro yelled loud enough to make the whole family turn to stare at us. "Damn straight! Who cares if I'm a superhero who occasionally fogs out, has trouble opening jars, carrying groceries, concentrating, orienting myself, or remembering my own name or what I had for breakfast?!"

"I am so with you on that! Fuck it if I wince sometimes when a spoon hits the bottom of a sink on the other side of the house. Who cares if a single touch during a flare-up can make me scream in agony, or that my digestive tract becomes a battlefield at the first sign of stress? That is apparently the way I was made."

Captain Grief had suddenly sidled up beside us and was looking at me with a new appreciation, if that was possible. I ignored her and just kept talking.

"And so what if I don't break into purple polka dots every time I have a bad day, just so you'll believe I'm in pain and can decide whether you care or not. That's why they call it an invisible disability, you bonehead! And don't give me that bullshit about yuppie flu. My nervous system goes bonkers on me and you just can't explain it!"

"Amen!" Captain Grief declared and smiled at me. "Say, you have that on top of grief brain?" She said it more as a statement. "So I may have x-ray vision, but remind me when you're having a flare-up, cause how the hell would I know." Captain Fibro gave her cousin an approving look. "That way I'll know to take it easy on you, hypochondriac."

Captain Fibro punched her cousin hard and Captain Grief landed in the hedge and groaned and could not or perhaps did not want to get up again.

"Say," I continued, "have you ever gone to Capes and Birks? It's my favourite lesbian superhero bar."

"I've never gone, but I've always been curious." She smiled and looked at me a little mystified.

"Oh, you'll love it. Trust me, you have no idea what you're missing ... yet."

Suffice it to say we all totally understood each other. Good thing, for a book with so many alter egos! Perhaps that's just the work of life, to take all your parts, similar or dissimilar, and realize they make up a whole being. Denying any part of that whole creates pain and fragmentation.

Change is loss and I experienced it even before my dad passed away. It was a loss of identity — and I'm not talking about the kind where your credit card is swiped and someone charges a Lamborghini on it. I'm talking about the kind of loss that happens when you're on vacation skiing with your family in what you assume is your healthy body, but by the time you clip into the boots, shoulder your skis, and get to the top of the mountain, you're in so much pain you're already done for the day.

It's the kind of loss where you withdraw yourself from a dance class that has been your lifeline to the theatrical expression issuing from your very core. The kind of loss where you walk into school as an energetic twelve-year-old and hobble out again at the end of the day looking like you're ninety.

Change derails you from a set of comfortable, enjoyable, or familiar expectations you have for your life and what it will look like. I never knew how much my activities were a reflection of my identity until those outlets were no longer available to me. This begged the question, *Who am I if I can no longer do those things?* It's a hard sell to believe you're still the same person at the core when you don't recognize yourself in the mirror, or in your life.

Things improved greatly when I learned how to manage my symptoms, but I never really wanted to acknowledge that I had fibromyalgia. When I was young and I had not yet bounced back from my diagnosis, I wrote about fibromyalgia like it was an arch nemesis, a monster, or a villain. Captain Fibromyalgia is one powerful lady, and when Dad died, I began to go downhill—and my symptoms spiralled out of control in third year.

I enrolled in the Fibromyalgia Day Program at the University of Western Ontario. The package they sent me contained literature on grief. I didn't want the symptoms to be a part of me because, if I accepted I had fibromyalgia, I would have to stop demonizing it and be okay with the fact that this was just part of my identity.

After I was diagnosed, I sank into a deep apathy and convinced myself that I no longer cared to create anything ever again. But with the help of an ecumenical counsellor, I finally started to talk about my dad, and with the team at Western, I started to realize that the only way I was going to get along with this playmate would be to accept it.

This realization has only grown since I found my way into the holistic world, and my experience with chronic pain, loss, and bereavement is why I am a healer. It's also why I am an artist. Because I have a vital need for expressiveness, and I know I must never stop creating or I will literally make myself ill.

Loss never feels like a gift. But it is, in fact, a difficult opportunity to get to know yourself very intimately.

I have come to understand that the gift of empathy that I have is tremendously valuable to others and to myself. In many ways, I feel like I'm here to help others come to terms with loss and be more comfortable with death. I'm also here to learn to appreciate the difficulties of self-acceptance and to see the things in life that slow me down not as obstacles but as speed bumps that force me to take care of myself.

So, to Captain Grief and Captain Fibromyalgia, I say thank you for showing me my greatest strengths. As for Lieutenant Lesbian, who I didn't get to meet at the picnic, I salute you as well! She was so straight she didn't recognize herself in the mirror until 2005 (when I was a 27). Talk about invisible parts of yourself! It's worth the risk of changing to become visible! Thank you all for being honest with me and for allowing me to accept myself and understand what it is to be seen. You made me who I am.

CHAPTER SIX
GETTING ON WITH IT ISN'T GETTING OVER IT, BUT YOU HAVE TO START SOMEWHERE

I remember someone told me a story once about a widow and how she could not bear to go to bed unless she was wearing her late husband's tuxedo. *What an absurd image*, I thought.

A woman lying in the dark, perhaps twisted in the sheets with a hard-won expression of slumber on her perhaps young face. Yes, it's so clear. Her small body enveloped in her partner's big black suit jacket, pants, and large white collared shirt with a black bowtie hanging like a necklace under her chin. At times, I have felt *that* desperate for comfort — when the only way to feel like the one you loved is around is to hold something that belonged to them, or let it hold you.

Such things become completely logical when you're sorting out how to be close to a person who is no longer here. On the eve of my four-year wedding anniversary, I don't mind saying that I was totally tempted to haul out my wife's tux, just to see if it would be at all comforting.

I was going to do that, but then I found the CD of our wedding photos. Having spent the entire day in the wading pool in my living room (remember the one full of grief?), I was completely dehydrated and thus totally able to be transported by the pictures without tears. The feeling of pure wedding bliss was expertly captured and I was taken back to the joys and hiccups, the beauty and the wonder, the food, the music, the flowers, and to *her*, the one who was forever. It also didn't hurt that my wife and I loved challenging our photographer to take pictures while laughing. At one point, when I got a little overly sultry, she actually had to put her camera down in her spasm of laughter.

Captain Grief came over to watch the CD with me, and she got a little snotty at one point, and not because she was upset with me. She reminded me that it was her wedding anniversary too. I started rummaging in the kitchen for some emergency anniversaries-kick-my-ass treats.

"Oh well, at least we're together." I smiled over my shoulder, reached into the fridge, and produced two Coronas. "Let's crack open some cold ones and vent over dinner on the deck. It's a nice night."

She smiled weakly as she reached into the pantry to grab the bag of chips and the chocolate cookies on her way out the door. I looked out the back window and watched her mouth the word *pizza* and do a shaky take-off. She flew off at top speed to Mama Amorphous's Authentic Alien Pizza in sector 14. Their outer crust is amazing, but the cheese is all over the place.

While she was away, I selected some mellow but not too depressing music, chopped up some veggies, mixed some dip, and went out to light a few citronella lanterns. Five minutes later, I was just plumping the cushions on the patio furniture when the Captain streaked back onto the deck and opened the puce-coloured box that was shaped like an asteroid.

"Hot as the sun; fast as a shooting star." She presented it with a flourish and a perky attempt at their tagline. I popped open the beer and handed one to her. She kicked off her boots and sank into the chair opposite me, under the ivory silk tree, which I noticed looked more bridal than I would have planned.

"I'm shocked it didn't burn up on re-entry to the atmosphere," I said wide-eyed.

"The box is insulated with an industrial-grade flame retardant." And when I made a face, she followed with, "Food grade."

I shrugged and took a very warm slice of Hawaiian pizza.

"So, on a scale of one to godawful, how was the food at your wedding?" she asked, her mouth full of cheese.

"It was fantastic, actually. We both had trouble deciding if we wanted the chicken or the roast beef. And knowing how good the appetizers were, we were really conflicted between eating them or spending time with our photographer."

"Nice. Ours was pretty good too. She did every course in the form of a different tart." I looked at her with a furrowed brow. "Oh, it's a superhero thing," she said. "Take your bite to go so you don't miss out even if you have to relocate to save someone."

"Practical, I guess, considering the guest list."

"Magical, more like. Everything else was epic. Mortal weddings are so sedate in comparison. If weddings won awards, mine would get the Oscar."

"For best actress in a supporting role, maybe."

"Oh, please, there's no comparison. Ours was a destination wedding, with a legal ceremony on the side of a mountain in the Alps. Thanks to Switzerland for not being neutral on that point." She mimed taking her hat off and bowing in the general direction of Switzerland.

That's it, I thought. *I need to take her down a notch.* Our own wedding seemed to have been afforded legendary status as soon as it happened. We knew how to throw a party! "Um, wasn't your celebration briefly interrupted by a herd of goats and a very surprised, lederhosen-bedecked goat herder?" I smiled to myself.

Captain Grief snarled, "Hey! As soon as he was invited to the party, the guests got into an impromptu game of Catch a Goat, Kiss the Brides. Everyone was enjoying themselves, and I think he loved being our cake topper!"

"Well, I think *our* cake was beautiful. Our toppers were little mushrooms. And we had a pair of swans that *magically* showed up on the lake, and fireworks, and a kick-ass DJ, and *a sign warning of bears in the area.*" I ended on what I assumed would be an impressive note.

"You think that would have broken things up? Try a nasty supervillain sending you a Mixmaster with explosives and a note saying he had an elevator full of innocent bystanders, toddlers, and stuffed animals that he'd blow sky high if we didn't get there on time."

"You're so full of it," I scoffed.

"You wish. Bombs Away was pissed because he wasn't invited. It's a good thing the bridesmaids took care of him."

My mind travelled back to the close calls at our wedding, and I felt like our competition had turned to sweet remembering. "Yeah, it's vital to have outstanding help around you the day of. Like say, when your officiant loses your marriage licence and tells you the night before, on the dinner cruise you invited him and his husband to. Then, when he still can't find it on your wedding day, you have to gather up sufficient personal identification and your broom (that's what Kara called herself — you know bride *and* groom) and drive to the next town to purchase a new one."

"Yuck. Yeah, I remember you saying that." She nodded. "Thank God for the master of ceremonies and a good friend with a car. And fire extinguishers."

"Sorry?" I felt my skin goose pimple, my hackles raise, and my tendency toward competitiveness spring out of my body like the neck frills on those scary dinosaurs that shoot venom. "I hope you're talking about yourself."

There was pointed silence as Captain Grief chewed for a while. Then she said, "Well that shower of asteroids that caught us on our way to the honeymoon suite on Neptune totally came out of left field. My gown almost burned to a crisp. But now that we're talking about it, didn't someone burn their wedding speech to a crisp?"

"Mrrrrrr. Piss off, I just got a little close to the exquisitely decorated, candle-laden table. And FYI only a third of my speech was actually on fire. You know how exuberant my gestures can be." My wife had noticed, snatched it from my hand, and stamped it out in time, so it was all good.

"You is a spastic pyromaniac yes?"

"Shove it, Yoda."

"Please, you aren't fire resistant — I would have killed to see your face. That would have been hilarious!"

"It was an enduring moment!" I spat back. This was seriously reaching, but she paid no attention.

"Hey, can we time travel to see that? That would be so worth a good barf!"

"No. Since when are you pro-vomit? And FYI, the sprinklers didn't come on and the firefighters didn't show up, so it *was* all good."

"Bored now." The Captain, having consumed most of the pizza, put the plate of veggies on her stomach and stretched out on the chair with her feet on the table.

"Hey, at least I didn't end up having to catch a goat for each kiss. We had a kissing jar, and it was a dollar a peck for people if they wanted to see us smooch."

"Yeah, how did that work out when some smartass put in a twenty, huh, Sparky?"

"It bought a lot of beer. You can't buy a two-four with a goat." I snatched a carrot from the plate and crunched with contention.

"No, but the goat herder's family had a microbrewery and his mom made great schnitzel."

"Well the cottage we rented had a hot tub and we drank Caesars for a week."

"We did the backstroke in the Milky Way and discovered more alien life."

"You did not!" I didn't mean to throw my stub of a carrot at her, so I was lucky it landed in the begonias.

"We certainly did. They walked into the Irish superhero pub we *discovered* on Jupiter. They're crazy about the Irish. We drank all night with them."

"Wait, so there are aliens with Irish heritage as well as Italian?"

"Nah. I mean the Irish invented the little green men, not the other way around, but the aliens we met were just hardcore groupies, same as the ones with the pizza shop!"

"What?" I couldn't help but break my disgruntled streak and laugh. "You're full of blarney."

"Honest." She raised her right hand. "They sucked at cards, but they were pretty good at darts. And at the end of the night they started fighting in the parking lot because one of them had let the spaceship run out of fuel." I choked on my beer a little. "We let them get in a few good hits before we gave them a launch boost."

It was a good story and I was smiling. However, I knew there was one last big gun I could bring out to win our friendly competition. "Wow, that's pretty unbelievable."

"Thank you, thank you." She waved at a fictitious crowd.

"But I bet I can do better." She paused midwave and looked doubtful. "On our way to our honeymoon, we stopped in Wiarton to get a picture with the giant Willie … statue. It was big."

"You win."

"Thanks."

BE NICE TO HAMSTERS

I'm Captain Grief, damn it, not a book babysitter! I have a lot to do. I had to watch her run around the house in a frazzled panic muttering, "Okay… this is happening…" It was embarrassing. Although it must be freaky to realize that while you miss your partner like hell you also miss your old life and start to entertain the idea that you want and could meet your next partner. I'm not there yet, that's why I'm on the couch sweating just watching her get ready for her date—which I am *so not* jealous about—and drinking tea and laughing with nothing in the world to do, which I am not bitter about in the slightest (really I'm not). After all, I just saved a bunch of hamsters from certain death.

They were all innocently rolling in their little hamster wheels on the living room carpet, thinking of nothing but lettuce and wood chips, when an irresponsible owner left the front door open! They rolled right down the steps and into the street. Cars were swerving, children were screaming, neighbourhood cats looked hopeful. I heard the tiny rodents squealing for help from across town with my super attuned-to-helpless-victims ears, like they were squeaking through a megaphone.

I swerved through the street and rounded up all eighteen of them (who ever heard of a crazy hamster lady, right?) before they became fuzzy speed bumps. After I got home, I was so wiped from the rodents' brush with death that I cried on the couch all day. It's only now, after an emergency call to my bereavement counsellor, that I could drag myself to the computer and think about how to write some more of this damn book…

Excerpt written by Captain Grief

So, yeah, Kelly's been having a rough time being a single mom on top of all these other life complications going on, at the same time as chomping away at the grief monster one bite at a time. But I have it rough too! My job always seems to come first. It doesn't matter if I'm relaxing with a cup of tea in the bath, or pinning someone to the mat in my Superhero League intramural wrestling finals (I almost had her too), when I get that superhero call, I have to go!

Of course, even I need help once in a while. The other day, when I was bawling so hard I was forced to take off my mask and then my cape and use them as tissues, I got an emergency call about Dr. Zed. He had planted a bubblegum bomb at a seniors' home and was threatening to detonate it if they didn't hand over all their teeth. *He's a weird dude.* Anyway, I wasn't fit to fly anywhere. But I had to do something — anyone who threatens senior citizens is a piece of garbage.

So I called my good pal, Lady Twister. When she saw how laid out with sorrow I was, she hopped right on over. She detonated Dr. Zed's device, contained the bubblegum explosion in a windstorm, and swept up Dr. Zed and his army of evil mutant molar minions in a cyclone of pink bubble fury, leaving the senior citizens and their teeth intact. Then she had my mask and cape dry cleaned and took me out for a beer. Boy, I've got some super superfriends. I guess I do need to talk about them more. When I needed them, they were like an army coming to my rescue.

Kelly talks a lot about *her* friends, how they've been her heroes and jumped to help her time and time again since her wife passed. I guess that got me thinking about mine. I'm really lucky I have friends like Lady Twister. She picked dried bubble gum out of her hair for weeks after the fiasco with Dr. Zed. And not one complaint.

I can still save the world, but I guess I just need to slow down sometimes and take time off … oh.

IS IT JUST ME OR IS THIS HELPING?

Captain Grief was hitting a bit of a low this week and I was not. Last night I went over to her place and when there was no answer, I put my ear to the door. It opened a crack and I heard her crooning, "Noooooobody knows the sorrow I've seen, nooobody knows but … everyone." It was grief intervention time. Also, I was feeling good, so in a position to give a little back. I went into the kitchen and found her on the floor under a pile of Cheetos. After I wet-wiped the orange powder from her face, except where the tear tracks ran, I sent her to the Banff Hot Springs for a dip. When she returned, I served her macaroni and cheese (had to use up the piles of powered cheese somehow), meatloaf, and mashed potatoes.

After her second helping, she looked at me with a much less bleary eye, suddenly took in my overall content manner, and said, "What's up with you … sunshine?" I knew she was feeling better, as sarcasm runs her engine like oil in an army tank.

I shrugged. "I had a pretty good week." I cleared the table, went to the kitchen, and put on the kettle. As I did the dishes and told her about it, she sat perched on the counter.

"This wouldn't have anything to do with the super-girlfriend you've acquired?"

I ignored her accusatory jibe and said, "Yeah, but it's not just Amy."

Captain Grief started to mutter, displaying super–sour grapes.

I opened my purse and started rummaging. "It started with this card that Super Mom sent me." I pulled it out of my purse. "It helped, but in the way a quick tug on a Band-Aid stuck to a hairy arm helps." I looked down at the card, at the cubist-looking representations of angels, and read the text to her. I think she liked the idea of angels putting a few blocks in the way to make you pay attention and not miss out on life.

"Shit disturbers." Captain Grief chuckled.

"Seriously." I could see the fire refuelling her.

"It's a bit on the cheesy side," she said, "but it does the trick, especially when that's what happened to us. Come along and mess with *our* lives, will you?" She shook her fist at the heavens and looked like she was going to slip under another pile of Cheetos, roll around until she was orange and hope she was camouflaged enough to fool me into thinking she wasn't there, so I distracted her with cookies.

She took a nibble of one, slumped against the window frame, and sighed heavily. "Having your wife die certainly falls under the *uncomfortable* category."

I rolled my eyes and took a cookie. "But it does create an opportunity to think ... What the freak *do* I do now?"

"Punch inanimate objects," she offered.

"After that," I said. "I mean when the panic has passed, I think an answer usually follows."

"Which is?"

"Anything I want! I mean, I married the love of my life. Then I had a kid, and the focus of my life changed. And then it changed again when it was only him and me. Now, more than ever, I'm not sure what I would do if I didn't have the Ginger Menace." I snuggled into the couch. "After all this change, I realize the shaking up of things is becoming ... well, a *positive* thing. Even if I am having to remind myself that it is."

"Hmmm." Captain Grief was looking considerably more cheerful. "I've taken on some supervillains that my wife never got the chance to," she said. "And I inherited all her nifty super gadgets! And taking over her duties has pushed me to face some things I was ... a little scared of." She looked rather sheepish. "Ha, some superhero I am."

"But you did it," I said, splashing some milk into her Earl Grey tea. "Being brave always requires being scared out of your skull at the same time."

"True. You've run the brave gauntlet yourself, even if it wasn't an actual gauntlet."

"Yes." I sighed. "But I still haven't weed-whacked the side of the backyard that actually grows grass." When Kara was here, it was a field of green. "It's half jungle, half mudslide. I have to hose off my son every night."

"He'll live; it's just dirt."

"Totally. His clothes are all stained, but he'll be well exfoliated." I took a calming breath. "I decided there are acceptable causalities when you're frying bigger fish."

"Wow, you're looking pretty relaxed." She hopped down from the counter to peer into my face.

"Maybe that's because I feel like I've finally let go of my death grip on life?"

She nodded. "Me too. It was like this tense effort all the time, to smile and be brave. Like after you rip a car door off and pull someone out of a burning wreck. I hate it when I can't stop bracing, even when I put them down, like I might have to save them again at any moment."

"I can see why you'd need to let that go."

Captain Grief dipped another cookie into her tea as she considered. "I guess you can't stay like that forever. Something has to change."

I nodded. "But it's a place to start. A scary place, but a place…"

The Captain took a bite of her soggy cookie. "So, what *do* we do?"

I took a deep breath. "Well, this week I took inventory of all these massive changes in my life. And I realized something. I have the chance to create a new and exciting career. I'm being more creative, and I gave myself permission to find some joy in my life." I started to feel a sensation that made me want to sit up straight and beam. Captain Grief looked at me with a side smile and then nodded like she hadn't heard anything. "I turned around and realized that the anniversary of her death is in *three months*. When I started writing my book, I never thought I would survive the Year of Firsts."

"Wow, that's big. So you just read the crappy card, thought all that, and went to Disneyland in your head?"

I heard her usual rough tone implying bitterness about my hiatus. "No. Last Thursday I was so discouraged, I didn't want to write anymore. And I realized, I needed to let go. To accept that life was going on — and that I was allowed to be happy about it. So that's what

I did. I cried, I wrote, I laughed, I yogaed, and then I took the Menace for a hearing test."

"What?"

"We needed to see if everything was okay. He loved the sound booth! But as we were sitting in the audiologist's office, I looked up at the wall for some reason and saw this little plaque that said, 'Happiness often sneaks in a door you did not think was open.'"

"What the hell does that mean?"

"That I did it. I was there. At a place where genuine happiness was. After all the time I spent panicking about how it would happen, it just appeared." I looked at her pointedly and when she didn't respond I said, "I felt like I could conquer the world in that moment."

"I know the feeling." She smiled and raised her polka-dot mug for a cheers.

*

Thanks to all my friends and family for reminding me that I don't have to be a superhero, but also that they frequently think I am. This is for you.

LAUGHING AT MYSELF

"Oh, come on, it's funny!"

That's what Kara always said, or at least said with her eyes. Even if I was scowling, even if I'd been crying, even if I'd been scowling *and* crying *and* threatening to hit her with something large and heavy, my wife always hazarded to laugh at life.

Before I met her, I was a tenser version of myself. I had come out only the year before, I was working off a string of intense relationships and emotionally transformative experiences, and I was building a framework for a healthier and happier me. In short, I was doing a whole bunch of crap that wasn't much fun, even if it got me places.

Meeting Kara was like the Universe stepped in and said, "Come on, woman, relax a little! You did the work, so pop open a beer and put your bloody feet up!"

Kara always encouraged me to write. She gave me a journal inscribed with the words *To the best writer I know*, and we always knew how to get a laugh out of each other. The memories are still laced with joy. For instance, whenever I wear her monkey-eating-a-banana socks, I laugh because I remember her wearing them with her tuxedo on our wedding day!

I laughed more with her. I learned to laugh at things that used to infuriate me. My decisions became simple. Kara came along at a time when I was starting to understand how joyful it was to follow my intuition. It led to her, after all. I was really challenging myself to be discerning about where I was putting my energy and why. It was easy to relax around her and see the naturally humourous side of life, and no matter what happened, I was always up to being a fool for that wonderful woman.

The running jokes in our relationship were more like marathons, and I began to categorize how funny she thought something was depending on her type of laugh. There was the smile and quiet chuckle that meant I got her attention enough to appreciate my attempt at humour. The rolling laugh where she slapped her knee, usually after slapstick jokes made in what I termed "her stupid movies." And there was the deep tenor two-pronged bursting out of her, "HAA-HAA, HAA-HAA, HAA-HAA!" — the reason I married her.

Once in a while, when I would really get her going, the laugher cycled through all the types, and when she didn't have any air left to laugh, she would wheeze à la Cookie Monster and clutch her stomach. That was so satisfying.

I remember the first time after she died that I truly laughed again and was completely overjoyed. I was curled up in my living room with a glass of wine and some good friends. My mother and I were telling a story about when Kara met my grandmother (who at the time was looking forward to her hundredth birthday). Actually, it was more a story about my grandmother and how she plied my mother with questions after meeting Kara, my new girlfriend.

Kara wanted to shop while we were visiting, so even though she had walked through the door in khaki shorts, a ringer t-shirt, baseball cap, and a buzz cut, Grandmom had dutifully looked up all the dress shops in the small Ontario town. Ugh! So my mom (God love her) very patiently explained to my grandmom that even though Kara was a woman, she did not wear dresses and she never would. Once Grandmother looked at Kara as masculine, she could never use the pronoun "she" for her without reservation. And when Kara's sister went into labour and we had to bust it back for the birth, I remember my grandmother's imploring words: "Kelly, *you can't* let him go alone. *You need* to get in that car. *You need* to go with him!"

She always loved Kara, who was apparently the best father and the best husband in the world. Even when my grandmother started to forget the world and many of the people and things in it, she still remembered my little family.

When I got pregnant, however, the internal understanding that Kara was in fact a woman, led to a little disturbance in the usually calm waters of Grandmom's world. Kara and I both Cookie Monstered our way to hysterics when Mom told us about her conversation with my grandma, which she re-enacted for my group of highly appreciative friends that day when I had my first real laugh after my wife's death.

"So, Kara *is* a woman," my grandmother said tentatively.

"Yes, Herta."

"And the baby isn't hers?"

"Not biologically, no, Herta."

"Because she doesn't have a ... woo-woo." She flicked her pointer finger quickly twice in the air to convey her meaning, and we all howled.

There were a lot of things about that pregnancy that brought out the best in my wife. Her caring, ever-ready, encouraging self came shining through. And this was not lacking in the few days leading up to the birth.

We nested like dormice, ate Indian food, and tried to laugh the baby out. He didn't dislodge himself. Maybe because he didn't want to interrupt the jokes. I remember sitting on my little meditation cushion on the floor, trying to calm him out, when my mother and wife came home with a copy of the book *All My Friends Are Dead* by Avery Monsen and Jory John. They rolled with laughter simply seeing my horrified expression.

The understated cartoon illustrations just got me. They are *highly* inappropriate in the most perfect way. My favourite pages sport a grim reaper saying, "My job makes me feel so alive"; a disheartened plant saying, "Please stop buying my friends if you are just going to slowly kill them" (of which I'm guilty); and a lonely tree who has been rejected by a squirrel, to which he replies, "This is my worst day."

When I'm laughing at myself, especially the deep, feel-it-in-your-gut laughter, I am home. Every time I laugh writing this book, I recapture a little bit of the happiness I had with Kara. I never want to stop laughing, as it really is the best medicine and much less expensive than Tylenol. Guess that's why I purchased *All My Friends Are Still Dead*, in which a disgruntled angel says, "All my friends are still alive. Jerks. It's super boring up here. I guess I'm going to go watch some living people showering." Priceless.

CREATIVE LICENCE

My wife was a very creative person. She was a phenomenal cook, she took stunning photos, and unbeknownst to many, she was an amazing woodworker and crafter who did beading and felting projects. The last thing she made was a tooth pillow for our oldest niece when she lost her first tooth. The Tooth Fairy thought it was so beautiful that she gave Ava the *purple* money (ten dollars!), which Kara's sister has cursed her for forever. My wife was a full participant in the world of kids, playfulness, and creative expression. She also supported me wholeheartedly in my own creative endeavours.

And so, in September of that first year, I decided to let go of what I *should* be doing and just did what I wanted for a few weeks. I could say the reason there were dust balls the size of my head in the living room and dishes piled in the sink was that Captain Grief took me snowboarding in the Alps, and I got a little overzealous and tried the half pipe, knocked myself out cold, and woke up in hospital a few days later thinking I was Big Bird, but I'm pretty sure you wouldn't believe it. I could say that she drugged me and had to airlift me to an undisclosed location for a top-secret mission, where she needed me to play the part of a mascot. That might be a little far-fetched as well, *even though that really did happen.*

I could also tell you the reason I didn't add any pages to my book is that I had a major case of writer's block, which is partially true, if the block was bottles of beer getting in the way of the keyboard, and my eyelids blocking the screen after all the late-night hours I kept. I was having too much fun to stop socializing and sit down to write.

Hallelujah!

It was more than that though. I may have gone to a party or two, and I laughed at myself a lot — and that took me light years from anywhere I thought I might be when I was newly widowed — but in fact, some major creativity went on during those weeks.

Creativity has played a massive role in balancing grieving the old and embracing the new. My creative licence in this case called for glue sticks. Of course, Captain Grief wanted in, so we did something together. I've always lacked confidence in my ability as an artist, even though Kara encouraged me adamantly. I have not consistently been able to free myself from the voice of critical self-doubt when I paint and draw, not like I can when I write. However, the need to create visual art is insistent and alluring. More specifically, I had a new and empowering project in mind.

When I started it, I had a question to answer. What to do with all the *National Geographic*, *Real Simple*, and *Today's Parent* magazines coming into the house in my wife's name? I decided to get through the piles by searching through articles, cutting out the juicy words, making poetry, and letting go of the rest.

I love poetry. The way it looks, the way it reads, and the immediate images it evokes. I have always looked at scrapbooks, journals, and collages that include poetry and sighed a poor-speller's remorse. Scraps of paper with script in the poet's handwriting next to photographs and drawings seemed to taunt me and say, "You could never do that." I let my horrid spelling and grammar hold me back. I didn't want to write something I couldn't edit. But then a found-poetry exercise I did with my writing coach helped me break through that excuse.

One night, sitting around her table, we did a fun warm-up with a photocopied page from a gardening manual. It was absolutely freeing to escape from the tyranny of my inner critic, and I forgot all about making a mistake.

Now it was just about playing, having fun with language. Here's what I came up with:

ALPINE

mountain tops under a hand

summits of smooth limestone slopes,

usually barren slender thickets, blossom

where they join, Woodlands,

tiny leaflets bending willowlike,

New found land.

near the coast.

south.

As I reread my work, two things occurred to me.

One, *this poem is turning out really dirty!* (Who knew gardening could be so naughty?)

And two, I realized I could keep doing this if I wanted to! I didn't have to worry about spelling or grammar if I used something I cut out and reformed. Plus, it would give me the opportunity to do some accompanying visual art.

I began my personal project on a writer's retreat and all the lovely participants brought me scraps of paper and magazines, glitter, glue, and stickers to add to my scrapbook. It felt weird and freeing, and I almost had a conniption when I lost a very important word on the cottage floor, from a recipe I was using to create a poem about potato salad. I think there was sweat and swearing. I had to write it in and accept that this was not a project for perfection, but rather for imperfect expression. It was like messy, sticky, magnetic poetry, but more finicky, totally engrossing, distracting — and God help me if I sneezed.

I called my new project "Working With What I Got" and wanted to fill my sketchbook with poems. As I found more articles with subjects that were relevant to my wife or grief or our marriage, I plucked them out and went to town. And I found an important tool to remember when I'm giving myself permission to take creative licence: *If my inner critic is telling me that this is a waste of time, I know for sure I'm on the right track!*

And if you think I felt a little bit like a serial killer cutting out letters, you'd be right.

Captain Grief agreed. She was looking at the poems and confessed she didn't think she would have the patience.

"Sure, you do," I said and elbowed her, producing a bruise on my arm. "If you don't want to cut out whole articles, just find some pictures you like and thumb through the magazine until you see words in the ads."

It was actually in a moment like this that Captain Grief was born. A moment when I realized I was allowed to make choices and take creative risks. In fact, it was essential if I was going to finally let my creative drive be as big as my imagination. It was a necessary component of making me happy and expressive enough to heal. It has led me to many creative projects that make my heart soar like the eagle it has dreamt of being. Up here I can scream into the wind with joy and sorrow, and see that there really is a life out there for me rolling off into the distance, saying *You're in the air now, girl, flap!*

While I was safely in the sky and Captain Grief was in a wind tunnel with glue sticks, I decided to do an incognito time travel swirl and hope she didn't notice. I went to 2017 and found my project blossoming! I've made twenty-seven poetry collages. I've graduated from articles to whatever the hell I want — letters, horoscopes, a collage about Captain Grief, pages from my travel journal written in

Egypt, and most amazing of all, a poem created from the huge stack of sympathy cards I received at Kara's funeral — my most literal piece to date, where I transformed pain into hope.

I am learning the art of letting go as I create and I will continue to for the rest of my life!

There's another amazing thing too. I had saved a lot of articles on grief-related topics. But as I really got going on my found-poetry project, looking at those articles felt... uncomfortable — no, disgusting, actually — so I threw them out. And I started doing poetry on topics like transformation, forgiveness, spending quality time alone with nature and my creative practices.

I have collages about faith, my role as a parent, and my relationship with food. The best thing about it is that I'm not finished. When I take collages and art supplies with me, it feels like I'm carrying a baby and I'm already so proud of her; it's a project like this book, in that it has my heart.

My next poem is about Goddess Kali and her tough love lessons for being fierce. Oh, how things change and also stay the same!

CHAPTER SEVEN
HOLIDAYS CAN KICK YOUR ASS

I wondered what to get Kara for her birthday in September 2012. The woman hated surprises and couldn't wait to open a present to save her life. Even at her age, she still lay awake with butterflies the night before Christmas. Adorable! So I never stopped trying to come up with something unexpected. The question was, how?

One day I was cruising around on Facebook and saw the contest for vacation packages, I thought, *Nobody wins this stuff — but wouldn't it be cool?* Well, we did win. Yours Outdoors and Ontario's Highlands Tourism had teamed up to promote vacations in Ontario's beautiful north, with different packages to appeal to a cross section of folks. A yoga retreat at a lakeside resort sounded like heaven to me, but if this was going to be a vacation for me AND my wife, I had to look further than my yogic ambitions. And so I picked the artsy outdoors escape.

And that vacation turned out be one of the best memories I have of our life together. I wrote about it in September 2013, in honour of her birthday.

Journal Entry

This is the story of how she and I found ourselves up very, very high, on a suspension bridge overlooking the Haliburton Highlands...

"Oh, crap!" I exclaimed.

"What's wrong?" asked Kara, with a rather knowing look. She laughed out loud.

I looked at the gangly contraption before me. It seemed to spite me for the stream of gentle mockery I had tormented my wife with for the past few weeks whenever she thought about stepping onto it. Now that it was before me, slightly swaying in the cool fall breeze of the Haliburton Highlands Wildlife Reserve, I knew I was screwed.

In a lot of ways, I felt like our vacation had been building up to this moment.

The trees were green with hints of autumn when we left Toronto, but as we drove north they slowly turned. It was like we were entering another time and not just driving into the distance. We were also putting miles between the us that were parents and the us that was only *us*. It was novel and thrilling. The lodge we stayed in was shellacked to a highly polished gleam, and we were given a suite with a fireplace and a dazzling view of the lake.

That night we listened to the husband of the German husband-and-wife team running the lodge talk about the various attractions Haliburton had to offer. We dined with some seniors who brought their own wine (as did we), and feasted on an amazing wiener schnitzel. Captain Grief would be jealous.

Nothing but pleasure courted me when I imagined the little canoe paddle, the visit to the wolf sanctuary, and the short hike we would go on the following day. What I did not contemplate was the psychological challenge of one specific activity. It was a non-thought. What specific non-thought was that? *Two words: canopy tour.*

Before we reached the bridge, Kara took pictures of me practising, smiling and laughing, hooking and unhooking from a cable along a line of trees. Here we could learn to attach and detach the two safety cables to manoeuvre around the trees that the suspension-bridge course was strung from.

Kara was jubilant now that she could see the challenge ahead and size it up. She was always better with concrete fears. I, however, was absolutely excellent at denial.

But as I read the red-and-white warning sign at the beginning of the course, I could no longer deny my panic.

"Don't worry," the smiling, bearded guide said. "This bridge course isn't flimsy or shaky."

"Really?" I lifted my eyebrows. "You wouldn't call it a swingy, bouncy, wobbly-ass bridge way high up a tree that flies around in the wind?"

"No! This bridge is dynamic!"

Oh, good, I thought. *I'm going to pee myself on a dynamic bridge. That's so much more dignified.* I could feel my heart shuddering, my limbs trembling, and a fine layer of sweat forming on my back, palms, and forehead. I wiped it off my lip as I took Kara's hand and climbed up. I was shaking so hard, I could barely lift my leaden feet to go forward, and my arms made the too-low cables running along either side of me sway. The space to walk was just two narrow planks of wood, which swung from side to side as I tried not to look at the ground swirling beneath me.

I remembered that my own heights-challenged mother had conquered her fears (with the help of my Reiki master) to hike over mountains in Turkey. The mantra she used during her most harrowing moments sprang to my mind, and then, as if I couldn't help it, hissed through my teeth as I wobbled along.

"I will NOT be roadkill … I will NOT be roadkill."

It helped. Until my wife started to laugh … and take pictures … and talk about doing a collage of my apparently hilarious expressions and grimaces. I may have also screeched at her when she started walking/dancing backwards, filming me as she sang a song she had just composed, "Wilderness wife, wilderness wife, walking in the canopy and makin' all nice."

As Kara leaned out to take a picture of the earth below, every cell in my body shuddered like a million little creatures tucking in their tails. Everything on my body — my teeth, my hands, my arms, my legs, and well … my butt — was clenched tighter than a freshly pumped tire.

Another moment of humility greeted me when I remembered how I had scoffed a little when I saw the other participants, who were ten to twenty years older than us, and thought how we would whip through the course. Now I was bringing up the absolute rear and the guides were inwardly taking bets on whether I would finish or if they would have to turn me around and somehow get me back.

The farther I went, the wider the trees became. And a few times I didn't have the nerve to let go of the tree as I used my foot to feel for the next planks on the other side of the trunk. Kara had to clip me on and off the safety cable so I could keep going. I shouldn't have been surprised. The woman earned her wings in cadets by jumping out of a plane a hundred times.

"Yes," she often qualified, "but there was a boot on my ass every single time!" I guess we all need some help.

When we arrived at the little platform at the end of the course, I had never in my life been so grateful for a solid structure. Refuelling on granola bars and juice, I was finally able to smile for the camera as our guide took pictures of us together under the canopy of changing leaves. I held onto Kara's hand with such a fierce feeling of pride, gratitude, and gladness that we were here together. That we had survived.

Happy Birthday, my Love. Thank you ... for you.

SUPER IMPOSTERS

Captain Grief and I got into a heated discussion about costumes. It started innocently enough when I was trying to decide what I was going to be for Halloween. I suggested a black widow spider, but we thought that would be a little too on point. Ditto for a zombie bride or a mummy, which I wouldn't want to be anyway. I figured I might go with my standard: something with wings, glitter, feathers, halo, fuzzy ears, whiskers…

The year I was pregnant, Kara and I had great fun at Slack's (formerly Slack Alice — the only lesbian bar in Toronto) as angels. I was the quintessential feathery, fuzzy, halo-bedecked woman dressed in white, with a baby bump. It's a miracle! Kara was a fallen angel, of course. Pretty close to the angel from the Meg Ryan, Nicolas Cage movie *City of Angels*. Not just because she was the oh-my-goodness-I've-fallen-in-love-with-you-and-clipped-my-wings kind ... no. She was the angel who had literally fallen — on her face. Blood, bruises, black eye, bandages, maybe even a broken bone or two. We got some looks.

In the Year of Firsts, Halloween happened to fall on my writing day, so my plan was to decorate the house, write about it, hand out treats, take the Menace trick-or-treating, and eat his candy after he went to bed. So I wasn't sure if I should do more than a costume of a cold-looking mommy with a Thermos of tea.

The Captain, however, was going to a party — under duress. She found the whole Halloween thing very confusing.

"I fight evil villains and save people from terror every day, and there you civilians go, scaring the pants off each other for the fun of it. It's like the boy who cried wolf!" She crossed her arms with a huff. "People screaming all over town and they're not even in danger! I used to be able to handle it, but I'm a little off my game this year. And my supersonic ears get totally backlogged with all the fakers."

"Well you don't have to stay here. You could fly off to a desert island for the night."

"Nope, I already promised to go out. My friends say I need to get a life outside of hero work. It was either face the party or seventeen supernoogies and a few atomic wedgies."

"Yeah, but widows should never pass up the opportunity to dress up and have fun...and candy! You just have to find a costume you love. What about another superhero, like Xena?" I suggested.

"And be sued for misrepresentation? I don't think so."

I could tell she was taking this a bit too seriously, but I was unsure how to change the topic safely. "So I guess a police officer or a firefighter is out?"

"Humph."

"Well why don't you wear a bathrobe and a gel eye mask and say you're Captain Grief taking a night off? Then if you need to actually save someone, all you have to do is whip it off."

"Or find the nearest phone booth," she huffed. "What are you dressing the rug rat as?"

In retrospect, I should have known better. "Superman. He's one of Kara's favourites. Sometimes I thought she subbed in for the Man of Steel on weekends."

Silence. Super open-mouthed, twitchy-eyed silence.

I tried to think fast, to repair my mega-blunder. "She had enough Superman t-shirts to fill a Fortress of Solitude. And then we got the Baby Menace wearing them, and they looked so cute…"

"What?" she screeched. "You support superhero deceit? On this travesty of a holiday? How can you contribute to this mass distortion? The Ginger Menace can't lift a car off an innocent bystander or save a yodeller after a fifty-foot fall from a mountaintop!"

"He saved me." I tried to remain even-tempered as she spluttered at me. "And aren't we borrowing superhero status to write this book?"

"Well, that's not the point. It's all an illusion!"

"It's pretending you're a superhero until your own superqualities emerge."

"No. It's like when someone is screaming, 'Is there a doctor in the house?' and you stand up and say, 'Hey, I can take care of that.'"

I looked her straight in the eye. "You should be the first to understand that wearing a cape makes you believe you can do a lot more than you thought you could."

"I'm going to push you off a cliff right now and we'll see if you can avoid being roadkill."

"That's low."

"No, it'd be a real high one." She smiled. "You'd be a superhero imposter pancake. Plus, you could never pull it off. Get it, pancake?"

Those were fighting words. "I didn't want to do this, but now I'm going to—"

"You wouldn't dare."

"Yes, I would. I'm going to use my super-omnipresent author powers to prove you're wrong, that superhero status can save lives. Look at this!" The room started spinning violently, a little more than I meant it to, and the Captain didn't even have time to puke.

She grabbed the kitchen counter and steadied herself. "What is that? When are we?"

"2016. And *that* is a photo of me at Halloween that year. Aren't I fabulous?"

"You pulled rank on me — again?"

"It was the only way to get you to shut up."

"You sucked me three whole years into the future! To show me a photo of—"

"How happy I am."

Silence.

"How happy I am, not just because the Menace has finally shifted his long-time fixation on dinosaurs back to the world of superheroes, but because I'm revelling in the same world. I'm putting on all sorts of suits to see which one I like best."

"And you chose Black Widow?"

"Funny, huh?"

"Hilarious. You're lucky the Avengers didn't get wind of you."

"Oh, relax, this year is most fun I've ever had at a Halloween party, including the year before, when I let the Menace cover me in black marker and I went as the Paper Bag Princess in a leaf bag and a tiara. This is the whole point of this book, Cap. *We survived loss. We're having fun. We're going to have even more fun. Life is good.*"

No response.

"The Ginger Menace loves his Captain America suit so much, he's hardly taken it off. He wore it at the Bâton Rouge in the Eaton Centre. I had dinner with a superhero! And I was so proud of the shield I made him too. And that night, when I stepped out of the house all dressed in black with leather boots and my already curly red hair, I felt sexy and powerful.

"I couldn't stop myself from mind-melding into Natasha Romanoff. It felt so good, and I'd like to think I did Scarlett Johansson proud. I charged across the street checking for bogeys while Captain America secured the sidewalk. We stayed low and sprinted to the party unseen. Mission accomplished, target acquired. Candy. We have become an unstoppable and joyful team."

"You make me sick."

"Oh, come on, how is all of that not a good thing?"

"No. I mean…" She pouted so aggressively her lips disappeared for a moment. "Everything you just said is just so damn sweet, I might have to change my mind. You suck."

"I suck because I'll forever be grateful for you and the world of superheroes for reminding me that I'm strong and smart and resourceful and powerful, and I don't even need the cape."

"Stop! You're gonna make me cry! You're gonna make me barf! You're gonna make me cry and barf at the same time! I was on a two-hour no-tears streak. I'll get you for this!"

So it kind of went from there. To cut a long story short, we fought. Her sonic-boom yell took out all the leaves still clinging to the trees in the backyard, and I threw a plate of carrots at her head. She punched the kitchen sink, leaving a big dent, and ended up with baba ghanouj in her hair.

I told her she could hand over the chocolate if she didn't like my methods of persuasion, and she stomped through the front door before she opened it, leaving a Captain Grief–sized hole. She did call her carpentry contact to come over right away, which was thoughtful, but he arrived with a nasty note from her. She said that if I ever transported her through time again, she would strap me to her ceiling fan by the cape and turn it on — so I could see how it feels to fly.

Well, you can't win them all, but that night, I won.

After the carpenter left, I hauled up the massive box of decorations, including a little mummy that danced to "Thriller," cobwebs, tombstones, skeletons, and a number of large and scary critters that crawl all over the front of my house. Halloween was a big deal to my wife. She was also a horror movie and zombie lover extraordinaire. She was completely into *The Walking Dead*, which, after a few episodes, I refused to watch. Once we moved into our first house, she had aspirations of being the talk of the street in October.

But with Kara being so ill the year before, the decorations didn't all have a chance to make it out, so I felt I owed it to her to do it up proper. That said, I did have reservations about putting up the Grim Reaper. It seemed even more inappropriate than the black widow spider.

Whenever I looked at my wife around Halloween, I could see the haunted house in her eyes — the cobwebs, the bowls of goo, the pranks. In university, there were ongoing practical-joke wars between Kara and her pals, who were mostly dudes. My wife was certainly a victim as well as an active participant. I queried a good friend and former roommate of hers for additional evidence and found out that Kara and her industrious friends had sabotaged a professor's car by removing its tires, putting it up on blocks, and giving it a toilet paper treatment. Apparently, they also liked to randomly glue pocket change to coffee tables to see people try to pick it up. Since they threw a ton of parties, the parade of people through their house must have made this a running gag.

Another time, she and a pal lined the mouth of a beer bottle with Anbesol (a topical oral gel) and gave it to a friend from Newfoundland. He immediately spat and dumped out his beer, and the numbness in his mouth didn't wear off for hours.

"Imagine someone with a Newfie accent talking with a numb mouth. That one had us in tears," her friend said. *I believe it.* And Kara, being a Cape Bretoner, probably did impressions of that one for weeks.

The same friend also said, "There was a baby seal poster in our living room. Kara and I ... modified it, with some craft paper. We added blood pools, X'd out the eyes, and put in a club. That cute poster was a Greenpeace nightmare."

Kara loved pranks. She told me that one night she snuck into her roommate's bedroom with a toy, or perhaps I should say, part of a toy. Something creepy with blinking red eyes. Kara tore them out of the figurine and hid them under the bed. The roommate turned off the lights and got into bed, and it was then that she noticed them. How did she see the evil red winking eyes, you might ask? *In the mirror opposite her bed, blinking back at her.* Apparently, they could hear the screaming all the way down the hall. Nice one, Kara. I'm glad I didn't room with you then.

That said, I did watch a roommate of mine hanging a *Blair Witch* stick figure outside of someone else's bedroom window. I guess university can be just as cruel as any other part of education. However, after the victim screamed herself silly, she was impressed with the engineering of that feat, so we couldn't help it, we had to laugh.

IF IT AIN'T BROKE

So what does a widow do a year after her wife has died? Well — and I can only speak for myself — I assessed things. What's left after a year of scrubbing the toxic emotional waste of grief out of my body? Which little corners are still collecting the pond scum of loss? Where are the cesspools of seclusion that I'm still in danger of falling into?

This is where, in order to explain to you how I tried to get through this, I have to stand by my identity proudly: *I am a weird hippie freak.* I work intuitively through the tasks of life, as well as in my creative and healing pursuits. I am a holistic healer, and I practise reflexology (ironically, a technique for detoxification) and Reiki (a form of Japanese energy work). I practise on myself every day. The people who know and love me often attribute my ability to process and meet the challenges of moving through grief to this self-care. To sum it up, *I aspire to trust myself, my wisdom, and my intuition, as well as the process I am working through, and I will continue to process this work as grief is for as long as you love them.*

That first year without Kara, as the date of her death (Remembrance Day) drew nearer, I experienced some serious anticipatory stress. And I spent a lot of time trying to figure out how far I had come and where I still needed help.

As the Universe often does, it decided to help me out by adding a little extra pressure at that time. Not only was I as sick as a dog for the better part of two weeks, but the Ginger Menace picked up a case of hand-foot-and-mouth disease at daycare. At first I thought it was just the too-much-pizza barfs, but the fever made me pause. I quarantined us for the worst part of the contagious stage. I shuddered when he touched things, and I wiped everything down with an antibacterial cleaner after he went to bed. On a positive note (which didn't totally help me), he didn't seem to care that he was an infectious plague-bag. He was his normal, spunky to wrangy, let-me-out-of-here-so-I can-touch-things-at-the-park self.

Suffice it to say, I majorly readjusted my priorities, one of which was trying to avoid a total mental and emotional breakdown. That didn't work so well. I was despondent, raging, negative, pathetic, and of course, crying my face off. So what's new, you ask. How is that any different than the regular wading pool I splashed into when grief came in the form of a tidal wave? Well you know when you get all perky and productive and make a list? In one of those moments, I made one the length of both arms put together, and since I was home long enough to work through some of the easier stuff, I got to the more difficult items, which were scaring the crap out of me. And, because of my self-care efforts, I was able to skip along the rainbow trail much further, in between tripping over something and being laid out flat on my face in the dirt. So the periods of suffering tended to feel much more potent and debilitating.

That October, I finally watched my wedding video, and then I cried on and off for a good forty-eight hours. My eyes stung like angry hornets' nests.

Super Mom was in Australia, so I called my Reiki master, Alison, who henceforth will be called Super Reiki Queen. She has a number of superpowers, including a calm voice, deep wisdom, emotional intelligence, and a steadfast allowance for the human condition and its natural foibles. She tends to deflate the panic. She talked me down, helped me reframe my perspective, encouraged me not to consider any of my emotions or needs wrong, and then she suggested *I break something*.

Come again? It stopped me short, even though I'd heard this story before. Apparently, the Universe wanted to remind me. When my father passed away, there was a nun at my school who similarly surprised my mother by saying, "There's going to be a time when you will need to break things, and when that time comes, come and find me."

Apparently, my time had come. This also put me in the position of divulging a secret. The tagline of this book is "Grief is messy ... own it" for a reason. I love order and organization. I may be an emotional packrat, but the stuff I pack is in individual boxes, labelled alphabetically. Maybe that's why I am so intrigued by the idea of *mess*. The choice to lose control is so freeing, but I find it very hard to implement. That's why Captain Grief was born, I suppose, to fulfill a deep desire to get messy.

"Do you have a brick wall?" Super Reiki Queen asked. She then proceeded to tell me all about the thrill and satisfaction of lobbing a glass vase at a hard surface and listening to it bust into a million pieces. She was quick to follow this suggestion with a little sage advice, "Just wear goggles and long sleeves."

"Well, when Kara first died, I was talking about having a plate-smashing party, but a friend suggested I put them in plastic bags so I didn't have to clean up the mess."

"Oh, no!" Super Reiki Queen objected. "That takes away from it. You need the mess."

I guess you really need to hear the shatter and skitter of shards in every direction to be satisfactorily destructive. Another widow I know suggested a photo on a dartboard, which sounds effective and neat, but I think I totally agree with my Reiki master. I needed to hear something smash, which, when I thought about it, was not a surprise.

I'd been allowing myself to sing and using sound as a healing element on my clients in my Reiki treatments. I'd been singing constantly and experiencing a massive release of emotional crap that had built up in my throat and blocked my energy. And I'd just completed a twenty-one-day mantra meditation, acknowledging the power of sound and exploring vocalized chanting as a daily mindfulness practice.

I was past believing in coincidence, and at that moment of realization with Super Reiki Queen, I was totally unsurprised to remember something. There was a cracked dish in my kitchen that I had been saving for something. I wanted to paint on it or frame it, make it into something pretty and more polite. This was the last dish I had that belonged to Kara and me as a couple. When her older brother moved to his new place, I had packed up the rest for him, but kept back this last one. Now it was earmarked for annihilation.

So why would I want to break a plate and hear it smash? I guess that question is as good as, Why did you leave me? Why did this happen? How do I have a life again? How am I supposed to live without you? When will this stop hurting? Why aren't you coming back?

The kinds of questions that make particular emotions rocket to the surface. Like anger. Sharp-toothed, seething, howling, pillow-screaming, fist-beating, I-want-to-break-something anger.

Earlier that year, in a moment of exactly that type of anger, I'd beaten up a doorframe with a silicone cupcake pan. I'd been transported — and utterly purged of rage — listening to the satisfactory whip-like snap of the plastic against the wood. However, I also damaged my house, so I hadn't done that since.

That October, the anger had built up again, and I was starting to notice a few other things that had built up, like crud in the bottom of a kettle that needed to be scoured. And so, on a fabulous suggestion, I got out a Sharpie and wrote words representing that kettle crud. Here are some of them:

Desperation

Despair

Loneliness

Madness

Frustration

Shock

Pain

Anger

Judgement

Vulnerability

Rage

Isolation

Hopelessness

Anxiety

There are a lot of emotions to nibble on when you're grieving, and this is a mere sample. Of all the words that hit me that day, the ones that packed the most punch were *anger*, *judgement*, *vulnerability*, and *isolation*.

Throughout this horrid experience, I noticed that I, the extrovert, tend to become introverted when I feel emotionally vulnerable. But it's more than that. I never liked to get messy or go to pieces in front of people. I couldn't do group grief counselling when my dad died. But it was finally time to let myself be messy … shudder.

As soon as the Menace was down for a nap, I gathered up infectious hand-foot-and-mouth laundry and took it down to the now nonbroken, nonsmoking washer in the basement (because I am a multitasker). I told myself that if I couldn't find my wife's safety goggles, then I couldn't do this. In the piles of hardware, tools, extension cords, and all manner of workshop junk yet to be alphabetically filed, there they were. Perfectly cheeky and hanging on the board above the counter, where she had left them. They were even the cool ones, not the geeky, hole-covered, grade-ten science goggles.

So I donned the glasses and stood with that plate, looking at all the words I had written on it. I stood there, registering my emotional response to them, letting the emotion build up inside me like a stirring volcano. I asked my spiritual guides to help me cut my emotional ties to these words, to help me break away from them. And still I continued to stare at the plate and at the wall.

I was quaking inside. How could I do it? How could I throw a plate at a wall? How could I allow myself and my internal neat freak to let it rip and possibly cover the entire laundry room with sharp little death shards? I breathed and shook, and after a few moments of total disbelief, I chucked that thing!

Divine, divine, divine.

That nun knew what she was talking about! And so did Alison and my mom and my pro-breaking-stuff friends. And I could almost hear Captain Grief screaming encouragement in the background, "Yeaaaaahh! Go for it, smash it up! Wreck it! More, more, more!"

I looked down at the pieces. A large chunk had landed face-up with a full word on it. It was staring back at me like a pair of blinking red decorative eyeballs on Halloween. I felt my stomach drop. *Isolation.*

Hmmm. It had to go. I quickly put on my goggles, picked it up, and smashed it onto the floor. Then I couldn't stop. Abandoning any thought of using the larger pieces for some sort of thoughtful collage, I picked up the rest of them and broke them all into tiny bits.

And then I sat, calm and happy, with a cup of Earl Grey and a plate of cookies, utterly content. As I exhaled, I felt like I was breathing dragon fire, expelling the non-useful, the harmful, the painful, the bloody destructive emotions. And I was left with new thoughts.

After all that expelling, I was calm and thoughtful. And suddenly, I had more to say. I was spiralling into the core of something that I was starting to understand. I was grasping at something I had been trying to comprehend for months and now with my journal in reach I was finally able to say it. So I opened it up to a clean page and let it fly.

Journal Entry

It has passed. You have now been gone more than a year, but only just. I know my grief has changed, the feeling of debilitation is less, or less often, or less intense, or some combination thereof. I know there is more hope. There is more joy than there was.

When I look at myself I clearly see the "me" that belongs to myself as well as the "me" that belonged to you. When I look at myself I see the life that is mine — and the life that I had with you, but at a distance, which is getting wider every day that you are not here.

Sometimes I think it's a miracle that I can still recognize myself outside of a relationship, because for many years I developed a sense of identity and dependency on my partner. For this reason the isolation has been very healing in that painful, growing kind of way.

The only noise and turmoil I have to confront is my own. Turning inwards has turned the noise into music. The singular melody has encased me, clearing my space of emotional debris so I can witness the change and transformation in my life still sliding around under the surface of my cocoon.

In here, my attention has been drawn to a number of things, external things I had no idea about or didn't fully appreciate were a reflection of the internal changes happening in me and have yet to happen. When I was young, my father bought me a butterfly net so we could go down to the creek among the reeds and catch a monarch. We had discussed the marvelous migration patterns of this butterfly and I was eager to be a part of their story, if only as a momentary witness to their long journey south to Mexico.

My thoughts are caught up in these splendidly orange-winged beauties, the once-threatened species that was starting to recover but is now back on the endangered species list. Theirs is a lengthy process of transformation, the emergent miracle of their lives has been a throughline in my thoughts. How do they do it? How do they change from an unassuming life camouflaged in the leaves to an enchanting creature that can take to the skies? All the answers lay in the mystery of the cocoon.

When a baby begins to form, it is one cell, the size of a poppy seed, but when the yellow-and-white-striped caterpillar forms a shell around herself, she is already something. Where does she go? I know now.

She dissolves. She un-forms, *breaks down* in the most complete sense of the word. She is no more. And the magic of time and life recreates her as a miracle, and when she steps out into the world once again, she is new.

This is the combination of biology, instinct, and faith that creates and completes this mystery. Once she shuts herself in, her body slowly breaks down, bit by bit, body part by body part, cell by cell, and perhaps memory by memory to the state of primordial ooze. It is the only way she can rebuild herself, to commit to this isolation and surrender everything to the Universe.

I've been asked to commit a similar act of faith, to spend a year doing nothing but let everything change. To release everything I knew, everything I was sure about, everything I was afraid of, and everything I was afraid would never happen, in order to transform this life into a beautiful new reincarnation of itself. And once I finally understood the importance, the urgency, of this process, I looked in the mirror and said, "Okay. I understand and I'm ready. Break down."

WAITING FOR SANTA

The fact that November is the gateway to December is ironic cruelty. I had now lost two of the most important people in my life not only in the same month but also one month shy of Christmas. The additional ironic blow was that this holiday was the most enjoyable, cherished, and magical time of the year for both of them. Losing them right before the start of the season and "celebrating" Christmas just after they passed away was like sustaining a terrible wound and getting the bandage ripped off every day for a month, like a sadistic advent calendar.

In December 1997, I remember putting up the decorations in tears. I remember sitting at the dining room table wrapping presents in the meticulous way my father had taught me. He had been an engineer and preferred everything to be done with mathematical precision, even gift-wrapping. I can still picture him showing me different ways to fold the paper and create the perfect creases. The practicality of this lesson can't compete with its personal significance; wrapping gifts is still one of my favourite activities of the season. I even stretch it out to make the anticipation of Christmas Eve last as long as possible.

So there I sat, just weeks after losing him, wrapping and thinking of him, like I have continued to do at Christmas ever since, feeling him on my shoulder almost measuring out the angles. Then Mariah Carey came on singing "Miss You Most (at Christmas Time)," and I sobbed my heart out. I felt like Christmas would never be the same again. And I was right, it never was. There's been joy and celebration, gratitude, food, presents, family, but there's never been anyone else who could read *'Twas the Night Before Christmas* like my father.

Kara and he both greeted the holidays like elves, and even though they never met, I know they would have loved each other. They delighted in giving gifts and were very serious about their Christmas lights and traditions. On Christmas Eve, Kara would lie awake like a kid, with anticipatory sugarplums ricocheting around in her head.

That November when I lost her, I had already bought her Christmas gift, a telescope with an attachment for her camera. I had lunch with my sister as a red herring, so she could pick it up with me and take it home. So in 2013, I decided to give it to the Ginger Menace for Christmas because, as much as it hurt to see it, it felt even more unbearable to leave it still unwrapped.

December also belongs to other memories, such as the Santa Claus Parade. When Dad and Grandpa went off on a yearly trip to the cabin, Grammy stayed with us and we all watched the parade on television. It was on one of those weekends that my father passed away in the woods of Manitoulin Island. My comfort has always been that it was an instantaneous heart attack in one of the places he loved most.

That year, as I sat with the Ginger Menace, we made snowflakes and ate popcorn and waited for Santa, and I sniffled as usual. But in the midst of my sorrow, I realized something. Despite the personal significance of those activities, I was totally focused on my regret that Kara was not there to share them.

I called my sister and told her I had gone through the anniversary of our dad's death without thinking about it. She realized she had done the same thing.

"I guess it *has* been a long time," she said. Indeed. You could look at this as proof that as you gain distance from intense grief, it fits much more seamlessly into your life. But in that moment, I was still a ways off from that where Kara was concerned.

It's not surprising that the coming of the snow and the holidays depressed me that year. I wrote in my journal, *I have noticed that my heart kind of clatters down an emotional staircase when a new season comes knocking at the door.*

Something about the omnipresent change, pushing me farther away from the place where Kara and I were last together, brings on a feeling of panic. That said, December was a bit different, perhaps because I had practised surviving the holidays without a loved one many times. I was entering into a resigned type of acceptance.

When I went to my first writing group after Kara died, we did a found-poetry exercise (you know how I like those) and this sense of resignation even sprang out of the text we were cutting up. It looked like this:

FOUND POETRY FROM PERSONAL ADS

I feel winter becoming

40 below

avalanche

Christmas

I am a veteran

of holiday loss.

But what was I waiting for? I wasn't waiting. I was stalling. I didn't want the truth to set in quite so fast. I needed a spoonful of sugar, gingerbread tea, and some Christmas music to balance out the coming of what was now — again — a very changed holiday. I had things to look forward to. My short nonfiction piece about Kara was just published in *Beer and Butter Tarts*, and I felt like the artistic career I dreamt of and the life I was praying for would emerge with the New Year. So I trimmed the tree and mulled the wine. I decorated cookies with the Ginger Menace and watched the gleam in his eyes as he experienced the season afresh, as he danced and stomped in the snow saying (without his soother — finally!), "Me, me, me [Mommy, mommy, mommy], it's 'now!"

Journal Entry

I am waiting for a lot of things, but the more correct question has become Who am I waiting for? I may go on to love and celebrate Christmas just as much as I always have. Perhaps even more intentionally as a tribute to my father and my wife. But I feel like there's a part of me that will always be waiting for Kara to come home. Perhaps it's the same part of me that will always be waiting to be with her again after a long and full life. In that way, I know she's waiting for me too.

CHAPTER EIGHT
GRIEF FUCKS UP YOUR LIFE, BUT YOU MAKE IT WORK

Sometimes a mom *has* to get out. All parents feel that rough patch when your patience is at its end and you're one-toy-car-in-the-tender-arch-of-your-foot away from a complete mental collapse. When I arrived at that moment, I knew a walk around the block wasn't going to cut it. So I threw caution to the wind and made plans *before* I booked a sitter.

And then I was screwed. The tickets were nonrefundable. I had a killer outfit, and everyone I knew was attending the event, or attending to life. My cab was on its way when my last hope called in sick and I was standing with the phone in my hand and the sliver of hope that Captain Grief would pick up if I called.

She did and was there in a flash, of course. Not because she was obliging, but because she has the superhero speed thing. The Ginger Menace had had a healthy dinner to offset any sugar. The bedtime bottle was made and the Captain-friendly bedtime stories were selected. She shoved me out the door harder when it made him giggle, so I went with it. I figured that was much better than the alternative of screaming and wailing (from her, not me).

The next day, my head was only a little bit heavy, so I invited her over for tea and a talk. I set the Menace up with a bowl of Goldfish crackers and sliced apples. I was just turning on the cartoons when I heard the door protesting on its hinges as she hammered on it. I ushered her through to the kitchen table where steeped tea, some little sandwiches, and a plate of cookies waited. I *did* want to thank her for covering for me last night.

"Well," she sat down, "aren't we civilized today. I should have washed my pinky." She smiled.

"Cute." I rolled my eyes as I poured. "So thanks for watching the Menace last night. I really did appreciate being able to get out."

"No sweat. That's what *superfriends* are for," she said as she stirred her tea.

"Yeah, I owe you one, but the thing is…"

She was looking at me pointedly. "Get it? The *Challenge of the Super Friends*—now that's a great show. Thank God he took a break from dinos. Retro superhero cartoons are the only reason I watch your rug rat."

"Charming." I blinked. "I knew you were eyeing that DVD when you were here last. Well, I guess we aren't in a relationship to sugarcoat shit."

"Hey, that's a good thing. Just being honest."

"Yup." I nodded. "You put the brute in brutal."

"Nice." She smiled in the way we always did when congratulating each other for cracking a good joke.

"Anyway, he seemed to have a good time. He didn't scream and hide under the couch when you came in just now."

"Sucker."

"Pardon?" I said.

"I had a sucker in my belt. Figured it'd keep him occupied."

I stood up and looked at my son to see that the lollipop wasn't stuck to his forehead or up his nose. I quickly traded him for a kiss and an animal cracker and returned to my oblivious companion.

I took a breath and continued. "Okay, yeah, he survived, so thank you." I tried to look very pointedly into her eyes to communicate the gratitude I felt and pressed on. "But just so I know, what happened in the bathroom?"

She shrugged. "You were out of popcorn."

"Try to focus," I said flatly.

"Uh, keep your cape on, we needed snack food and all we could find was pudding."

"What's wrong with that?" I was trying not to let my frustration seep through, as I had to keep her talking long enough to make my point and have some fun.

"Have you looked at those dinky little boxes? The pudding mix in those wouldn't satiate a mosquito." She looked like she was about to storm down to the company and tear them a new one.

I tried to look like I sympathized. "So you…?"

"Flew to the grocery store for more…"

"Baaahh!" It was all I could scream as I envisioned the Captain flying with the Ginger Menace at the speed of light through the atmosphere, going via Spain on the way to the corner store. I was still frozen and spluttering when she cut me off.

"Relax, Tightly Wound. I put him in a Snugli with an emergency parachute. I know he can't fly yet!" Her expression plainly said *the absurdity, you nervous mother.*

"Oh, crap." Of course she knew that if anything were to happen to my child, I would throttle her, but it didn't stop me from wanting to vomit.

"It was fine. We made it back to the house and had a ball mixing in the milk and beating the hell out of it."

"Heck," I corrected with a glance at the Menace.

"That too," she smiled knowingly.

"Okay fine, field trip. Fine, extra snack food for the bottomless pit, but did you have to make so much?" *Now I'm getting somewhere,* I thought.

"Yes." She looked at me like I was dim.

I paused to assess her before I said, "And traditional bowls were out of the question?"

"The bathtub was the only place that much pudding would fit."

"Of course, silly me."

"It's okay, don't be hard on yourself. You're working with less." She took a condescending swig of an invisible beer.

"Uh, I had to get up at six today, and my chemical balance is just fine, thanks."

She waved away the thought and helped herself to a sandwich. "And while we're chatting, I wanted to ask, is there a reason Kara's retro Superman and Green Lantern action figures are at the bottom of the tub … in the pudding? They're originals from her childhood!"

She was half smiling through a mouthful of cucumber and bread now. "We thought they could use a mud bath."

"Whyyyyyyy?"

"'Cause it was funny!" She suddenly boomed out laughing, clutching her stomach while cackling. To prove her point, the Menace did a smaller, shrill imitation of her laugh, as if he hadn't been paying attention to the adorable puppies Grover was counting back from ten.

He jumped up, ran on tippy toes to high-five the Captain, and went running back to the couch, jumping into the cushions headfirst.

"See, he loves me." She tried to distract me, but seeing my unchanged expression, she continued, "Okay, Kel, they're originals, metal joints, made to last. Those things could survive a nuclear bomb. Not like the crappy plastic jobs you get now."

"I know you're right, but when I was scrubbing out the tub" — I paused to make my point — "I found them suffocating…"

"You know they're not real, right?" She was tilting her head as she assessed me, perhaps looking for any signs of alien abduction.

"*Suffocating* in an impossible layer of congealed pudding that I had to scrape them out of with the end of a toothbrush."

"You on a hygiene kick?" she asked, still sounding nervous.

"Look, there *are* things that belonged to Kara that I could take or leave, but not these." I dug the action figures in question out of my pocket and put them on the table. I counted five seconds of silence and I enjoyed each one with absolute patience. I could see the realization roll over her cranium and suddenly the ceiling was very interesting to her.

"Oh?" she said, unconvincingly.

"Yeah. You remember how she felt about Superman."

"Uh-hum." She still couldn't look at me and busied herself giving me a top-up. "Sugar?"

"And if I had done this to you…"

She let her hand with the sugar jar fall. I moved Clark Kent and Hal Jordan and sat them on the edge of my plate, so they were staring at her.

"You would have torn off my head for the sheer panic I caused if you thought I'd lost something belonging to *your* wife. I thought they were cute before Kara died, but now I've grown quite attached to these, writing with them perched on my monitor. So much so that I get a bit preoccupied when the Menace is playing with them."

"You freak if you can't find them, don't you?" she asked with her teeth clenched.

"Bingo. I sneak them out of his toy box when he isn't looking and put them in a safe place so I can use them to inspire me as I write about *you*. They're these new, very significant symbols since Kara died, and my son and I have been bonding over them. Telling stories of when his mama was little. I've even started to notice the Green Lantern symbol around me. That's when I know she's with me."

"Yeah, but you're weird like that."

I looked at her, letting my angry face rip. I smacked my open palm with my fist, hard.

"Shit, okay, yeah. But, you're—"

"Shut up! You're just as much of a weird hippie freak as I am."

"Am not. Before Kara died, she was already calling you and your friend Naomi 'the Ghostbusters.'"

"So why are you put out when I believe in signs then?" She finally met my eyes with snarly lipped silence. "Kara and I looooooved supernatural stuff. We even had hilarious conversations about how we might haunt each other!"

"You and all the hippie freaks suck. The only signs I believe in are the ones on the road."

"Fine. So let's just say I borrow your deceased partner's superhero mask and then take a mud bath? Funny then?"

"No." Her voice was suddenly small. "I wear it at night. It's the only way I can sleep."

"Point taken? Got anything to say to me now?" I sipped my tea, waiting, expecting a good splutter, which I got in spades.

"I um, uh … ha. I, uh … would like to … ewww okay … apology."

"Apolo*gize*." I smirked.

"Yeah, that. Can I offer you … one?"

"Thank you."

"Thank God!" She almost fell off her chair and grabbed the table, panting and perspiring. "Look at my pits! And I thought I was sweating yesterday when I doused the Incredibly Evil Match Girl."

"I know, I see you're still pretty singed." I feigned concern. "Take your unitard to the cleaners and wear the pink one I gave you for your birthday." I smiled in an even more helpful way.

"Uh, hell, no!"

"Uh, hell, yes." I got closer to her and whispered, "You may have skirted the apology, but the punishment isn't over."

She suddenly looked shocked and almost awed with admiration. "Fiendish!"

"Yeah, I've been learning lots about the retro supervillains by watching reruns. Mostly how to cackle and make puns. And yeah, I'm also *really* glad for the dinosaur reprieve. Though it's adorable to hear him say 'elasmosaurus' with a speech impediment."

"I like it better when he pronounces *apple* and *owl* as 'ah-hole.'"

"Of course you do." I rolled my eyes.

"Especially in public — so when are you inviting me back?"

"To babysit?" I coughed out some tea.

"No, to deworm your cat."

"Gross." Suddenly something in her expression changed again. Was that guilt? A long silence passed between us.

"You saw the DVD of *The Justice League*, didn't you?" I asked.

"Not *just* that. I saw you bought the Ryan Reynolds remake of *Green Lantern*. He's yummy."

"Yummy and Canadian." I wiggled my eyebrows.

"Blake Lively is pretty delectable herself." She smiled.

"Very true, but Kara was a diehard Reynolds fan. She always said he'd be the only one on the planet she'd ever switch for." I waited for her to respond.

"I didn't need to know that."

"Well." I hit my fist again. "I'm the Punisher!"

"Nicely done." She smiled like I had her.

"You'd never believe I mainly grew up on a steady diet of Wonder Woman and She-Ra."

"Uhhhh, yeah I would." She practically snorted.

"I loved Batman too, but I was so intrigued by Catwoman."

She looked amused but also like she wanted to smack me. "You're such a dyke."

"Ah-hole." Now I was ready to launch the real arsenal. She really did unwittingly put me through the ringer, so I figured she owed me.

"Burn." She couldn't help but laugh.

"Did you see that coming?" I asked.

"Don't get a big head about a good joke."

"No, did you notice?" I pointed my finger up to the ceiling and slowly started to rotate it.

"Um…" She gulped. "It's getting a little swirly in here. I guess you're still … mad?"

"Nah. This is just for fun. You happened to arrive at the TIME of day when I feel a bit scattered."

"You said four o'clock for tea," she said, monotone.

"Tea and time travel." I was delighted to watch her eyes bug out at this. "I just omitted the last part."

"Yippee!" She gripped the chair behind her as the wind around the table kicked up. "I'm really beginning to think this is a misuse of power!"

The Menace noticed the kerfuffle as a pile of his drawings was caught by the wind tunnel and went spinning up to the ceiling. He came running over and started screaming with laughter and chased after them like he was running after butterflies. I started to laugh as I tucked the action figures into my pocket.

It was really getting loud in here, and Captain Grief had to scream, "Got any other little tidbits of info on your abilities before the world switches to Dorothy mode?"

I smiled. "Wait till I tell you I talk to dead people." I did not raise my voice.

"What?" she screamed back, her body becoming airborne.

"Nothing," I overenunciated.

So, while Captain Grief was retching in the barn, I started looking around. Ben was rolling on the swirling pile of paper like a pig in a puddle. I took a sip of my Earl Grey, pulled out my journal, and settled back on my couch to reflect on the future I'd witnessed during my time travelling.

Journal Entry

So 2014 was big for me, but 2015 and 2016 have been unlike any other time in my life. I have become quite fearless, working though some major life speed bumps, and I'm a creative machine. I knew I could work fast, but I look back and I'm astonished at how fast I've taken flight.

I scored an acting role in a choral performance as a seriously angry activist (I know, such a stretch for me) and got to scream down an audience mid-applause. I started reading sexy poems at a local erotica production and did a guest appearance on a podcast. Mike Holmes and his Canadian HGTV reality series came to fix my house. Our episode of *Holmes Makes It Right* is called "Here in Spirit."

To round this off, I've been to Cuba, New York, and Egypt, and took to the stage as part of an autobiographical production called #HERstoryCounts as myself and as my spandex-sporting crusader. Please don't tell her because she will knock me into next Tuesday (for real).

Then, of course, there is my book. That it's written. I didn't wish or plan for my partner and best friend to pass away, but there are so many things that have happened that make me feel happy and brave and free, I don't want to take them back. I could never have imagined writing the things I have experienced. I could even say I don't know what life would be like if it were not for this change. *I am not just surviving.* I am living — joyously, creatively, compassionately, spiritually. I had no idea it was possible, but it is.

BURN

I need fire. Not like I'm standing over a trashcan rubbing my hands in fingerless gloves near the flame, though I have felt like that. Our first apartment had a working fireplace. It also had parking, two bedrooms, a dishwasher, laundry facilities, and a patio. We found it in one day. Kara and I went to look at it on a whim, and we signed the lease immediately. It must have been providence, as that winter was brutal.

The apartment was in a house on a corner lot, and while Kara was out shovelling for hours, I was inside, my chronically ill body bracing and shuddering at the intensity of the weather. Every time the power went out, I raced to the third floor and waited by the fireplace for the light to return. That winter I burned eco-sensitive fire logs that smelled like coffee and never crackled the same way regular firewood did. Regardless, that little room was my sanctuary, with candles, Kara's beautiful photography of the cabin, and a large mantelpiece that housed all my symbolic knick-knacks for my Reiki practice.

I recommitted to my yoga practice in that room. I became a Reiki master in that room. I openly acknowledged that I was a medium in that room. I prepared to become a mother in that room. And if my son didn't have other plans, he would have been born there.

The day after the caesarean, I figured I would do Reiki on myself to speed up the healing of this invasive wound. But when I put my hands on my abdomen, it didn't feel like a part of my body. It was like I was putting my hands on a stranger. So I waited and watched as the warm sensation of Reiki energy poured from my hands into my body, and then I felt my abdomen. The reclaimed part slowly returned to me and I felt whole and back in my body.

This calmed me a great deal — until we got home from the hospital, and my mother and my wife decided to step out for a moment to do errands. My anxiety redoubled thinking about being alone with my child for the first time.

What if something goes wrong while they're away? What if I can't handle parenting on my own? What if I'm not ready?

I paced in front of the fireplace doing Reiki on both of us, singing his lullaby and listening to the quavering fear in my voice. As I walked, the familiar cushioning of the carpet underfoot, this fear ebbed. I slowed as beautiful, warm energy ran from me to him and back again, and we were reconnected. I knew because suddenly, just as my body belonged to me again, so did he. And then he drifted off to sleep in my arms, and that's when I thought, *I can do this.*

As babies do, he grew quickly. After the surgery, I tried not to overexert myself, but he got heavier and the two flights of stairs didn't get any shorter, so we decided to move. We purchased a house without a fireplace. We found it in one day. It had gorgeous old-growth trees. Two stately Manitoba maples, two lilac trees, an ivory silk, and a simply breathtaking sister birch called us home in a way that only trees can. It was enough, but I did miss my fireplace.

That was the winter I started watching the fire channel. It may not have produced warmth, but it had the right sound. The random splintering and snapping I craved. Our son was nine months old then and newly walking, hand over hand, along a new sectional in the abundant space. We made it through the winter and celebrated a glorious summer in our new home. They say the first year of being parents is the hardest on your relationship, and we were no exception to the rule. I loved the house and I loved our family, but Kara and I needed to reconnect. I stuttered and clanged moving into my new role as mother, while Kara seemed to glide seamlessly from taking care of the other children in her life to taking care of her own.

In the turmoil of the role change, I had become a very insecure version of myself. Searching for my old identity in my new reality as a parent made me feel like I had lost the self I knew. This feeling was not figurative either. One day, I was passing the mirror in our bathroom and for some reason something about the movement struck me as odd. I turned slowly to look in the mirror, not sure what I was expecting to see. Instead of my face, I saw a jumble of pieces, like a puzzle moving and shifting on a computer screen, like I had passed by a window instead of a mirror and I was looking through it at someone else. I was looking through a window at some *thing*, and I was immediately terrified, witnessing something inexplainable. I clung to the bathroom sink, mesmerized, watching the shapes rotate and shift until once again the image became my face. Something needed to change. But as time passed, things did not improve this constant state of dysphoria.

After a fight one day, Kara went to the Toronto Zoo with the baby and her side of the family. I was in tears and guilt-ridden at declining the invitation, but I knew I needed space to try to understand what was happening to me, to us. I called my Reiki master and cried my horrifying revelations out to her. In her sage-like way, she reminded me that while Kara and I were a couple, I was responsible for only fifty percent of our relationship, and part of my fifty percent was taking care of myself, which I was not doing.

I couldn't blame Kara for that. She was trying to help but she was always so focused on what other people wanted and needed, she forgot about herself. That made me feel selfish. And it hurt her when people didn't take care of her the same way. Slowly, it had made resentment rise to the surface. She felt angry and I felt small, which was not a good combination. All the reasons I loved her had not gone away; it was me that was gone.

To begin dealing with this, I tried to forget my marital problems for a time and pull back into myself to acknowledge all the things I was responsible for. I needed to keep this to myself, to address this away from our stressful home life, in energetic terms as well as intellectual. What happened next was manifestation. Or perhaps you could look at it like Newton's third law of motion, as the reaction to my action.

It was then that I won the vacation for the two of us on Kara's thirty-fifth birthday, to go to the Haliburton Highlands in Northern Ontario. When we arrived at beautiful Heather Lodge, we had a gorgeous view of the lake and the slowly turning forest around us, an amazing room, and of course, a fireplace. Kara headed off to get a fire log and I tried to relax.

Later, sitting in the light of the fire, I confessed my feelings, that while I was glad about the life we had, I regretted that we had both sacrificed things personally and as a couple to attain them.

I wasn't sure what she would say or how she would feel about my revelations, but gazing hard into the fire, she slowly nodded and said, "You didn't do this, we did this."

I felt a deep sense of gratitude. And over the next few weeks, that wound between us had a chance to regrow a thin, silvery layer of new skin. Though this didn't protect me from losing her. When she was ripped away from me, the wound was torn open once again, and I was left to heal it all over.

A small part of me wonders what it would have been like if we had not gotten that opportunity to reconnect. And sometimes I wonder if it would have been better if I could pretend that *the broken us was all there was*. Maybe it wouldn't have hurt as much to give her up.

After our time at the lodge, we fell into the routines of our new life. The house needed work, so Kara took some vacation time to get it done. I remember the day. I was finally able to write about it years later.

Journal Entry

It had been raining and the colourful leaves were soggy and sticking to the sidewalk. Ben and I went to a fire station with the Early Years Centre. We took the bus down, only to realize that the group was getting ready to walk all the way back to a fire station at the beginning of our bus route. I stepped into the fire station tired, irritated, cold, and in a deep pain that the damp and the walk had brought on, but when I saw my son's eyes turn into little proverbial flames seeing his favourite vehicle, I couldn't be cross.

We returned muddy and happy, and Kara had moved on from trying to get into the attic to recaulking the tub. It continued to rain, and the calming noise of the weather mixed with Kara's work set me at a strange kind of ease. I put on *The Wizard of Oz* for Ben and made a mental note of the day and all the firsts that I was sure would come.

Kara was three days into her work-cation when she started to feel sick. She'd always had respiratory issues, including all-season allergies, a structural defect in her sinus cavity, and recurring bouts of pneumonia and bronchitis. So everything was "normal" — until it wasn't. Until it was scary. She spent a day and almost a night at the hospital while I worried at home with Ben.

I knew how bad it was when Kara's aunt phoned me from the hospital, having arranged for her daughter to take care of Ben, and was coming to pick me up. I wore my new running shoes, the ones that offended my sense of aesthetics, but Kara insisted that we purchase. Not knowing how else to prepare for whatever was to come, it seemed like the only effort I could make that would have any impact on the outcome of the evening.

I'd been making an effort to depend on my intuition for information and clarification. Now came the time for it to serve me. It happened on the corner of Mortimer and Coxwell, outside of Toronto East General Hospital. Kara's aunt stopped at the red light and everything else that was happening in the world stopped too. Suddenly, it didn't seem real. There was this bone-deep, or even deeper, sense of peace. Everything was quiet and calm, and I remember thinking, *My wife is dying. I don't want to be calm. How can I be calm?* I didn't have to search for the answer. I was at peace only for a moment so I could get the answer: *She is going to die.*

I paced in the waiting room, not able to sit, and finally retreated to the bathroom to call friends. I knew I would need them and perhaps would be unable to reach out later on. The tall, skinny doctor with dark hair came to talk to me about moving her to Toronto General. The life support there was better, but in the end it did her no good.

A small and virtually undetectable bacteria called blastomycosis had made its way into her system and was wreaking havoc, shutting down all her bodily systems. Mould is not treatable by any antibacterial or antiviral agent, but we didn't even know what caused the pneumonia until we received the autopsy report. In the end, she didn't even have any viable tissue for donation.

All I knew was that her body was done. She took her last breath before she was intubated that night and did not wake up. Early the next morning, November 11, 2012, after a Herculean struggle, she was gone for good. Someone led me away from her. I didn't know where my own body was, but it followed hands I couldn't feel. At the house, I crawled upstairs and crept into a bed that still smelled like Kara. I'm not sure when I noticed it, but I quickly became aware that I couldn't control my body temperature.

I had never experienced shock like that before, and for a week I lived with a continual chill that ran through my body, all the way down my limbs. It was accompanied by a nearly continual tremor, mostly noticeable in my hands, but it began in my spine and travelled in every direction.

Winter was coming on fast, and the house around me was a beehive of activity that seemed to be running itself, even though it was far from it. A massive community and family mobilized around me and stoked the warmth back into my body.

I can't recall the exact night that it happened, but even with the support around me, I realized I needed to remake my sanctuary.

As the snowing and the blowing came in, I hunkered down. One night, under a fuzzy blanket with a cup of Earl Grey, I turned on the fire channel and found the psychological comfort I'd been searching for. This particular moment in time was about the fact that I was present, breathing, and happy to be in my body, and aware that something felt pleasurable. Perhaps it was the way the fire flickered on the walls when I turned out the harsh overhead lighting. Perhaps it was the sound of the crackling and the way the logs burned through and randomly clattered to the bottom of the fireplace.

For a few minutes, I had found a way, however brief, to be okay. I also knew that if I could find a way to be okay in this circumstance, then I could find a way to be okay again, no matter what happened. Soon, I was participating in this ritual every night, and I loved bringing family and friends into it. I knew myself to be a healer, but it was a while before I recognized that I was healing myself and others in these moments.

KARA SENDS ME A PEACOCK

I was not raised in a religious household. My mother assures me we sang "Happy Birthday" to Jesus on Christmas morning, but perhaps that was overshadowed by the presents and the chocolate and the gingerbread. I didn't feel that void of spirituality until my father died, when I asked my mother if he prayed. And so, when I studied Reiki (universal energy) for my fourth modality at college, I found the companionship, understanding, peace, and comfort of ritual—and a connection to God I had never know before.

On my first visit to my Reiki master after Kara died, where I'd spent most of the session in a constant stream of tears, she assured me — even though I already knew — that Kara had been with me from the moment she left her body. She was in a place where she was happy and unattached to the struggles that we experience on Earth. She still had work before her, but I understood that her work was now in a different place.

My teacher and I worked with shamanic aspects of spirituality, such as totems, the instinctual wisdom of animals, and the natural world. She once told me, "Kelly, you don't have totems. You have an ark!"

I had noticed peacocks quite a lot in my world the year before Kara died. When you work with totems, the energy is simple and straightforward, like the instincts of an animal, or what may be called the wisdom of the animal. And when energy comes in the form of an animal, it's always communicating a simple message and will just start popping up around you in the things you see and hear. For example, in billboard, art, illustrations, conversations, or songs. And mostly the oracle cards, of which there are so many kinds. The first deck I bought, on my honeymoon, was an Animal Totems Oracle. I knew I must get it as there was a cougar table stand at our hotel, a bear statue outside, and our rental cottage was plastered with photos of wolves. They were the first three totems that presented themselves to me!

Like the lion card that came up before Kara passed, telling me there was a period ahead of me in which I would need courage. And the owl eyes I dreamt of on the face of my grandmom before Kara died, their wisdom telling me *Pay attention to signs*. When an actual owl flew through the backyard on the day of Kara's funeral, right in front of my mother, in a flash a dream about my grandmother came back to me, and I understood the sign I was being asked to pay attention to. The dream had inferred that Kara would not outlive Grandmom. It was Kara's time. In that moment I knew eventually Kara's death could make my faith stronger. Eventually. If you ask, you become aware of ways to connect and you do get a response.

As for the peacock, she was around too. Before the weather turned wintery that fall of 2012, Kara and I had been lucky enough to receive tickets to a Cirque du Soleil show where the design esthetic was peacocks. On a trip to High Park Zoo in Toronto, Ben and Kara had procured peacock feathers to give me as a gift.

So we hauled out my teacher's trusty copy of *Animal Speak* by Ted Andrews, and read that this was the bird of transformation and eternal life because it most closely represented the phoenix: fire, transformation, renewal, burn. It was like the Universe was priming me to communicate with Kara by what it brought to my attention. Years later, I was quite tickled to hear that a peacock escaped the High Park Zoo and was flying all over west Toronto. There's something mystical about that bird.

It was only after Kara was gone that I realized, when she and I were in a particularly important conversation, there would often be a peacock around in some form. Like the day we were in an art shop we loved, and Kara was encouraging me to be brave in my creations, and I saw a greeting card with a peacock. The quote was something about your loved one seeing all the good things about you—the things you don't always see yourself. I thought about that greeting card a lot. It made me feel better about myself and also helped me acknowledge the slow transformation happening in me. I was learning to let go of a lot of things I didn't want to let go of. Soon I began to detest self-imposed limits and old coping habits, and I started to work through them.

I began to feel the need to be visible as a writer, so it was not an accident when my writing coach offered me as space in her blog-writing workshop where I created Captain Grief. I battled the most difficult year of my life with honesty and humour. *Animal Speak* described the sound of the peacock as a gurgling kind of laugh. It's interesting, as in many ways it was laughter that transformed me from a confused, scared widow to a woman with a mission to be an artist, to be a parent, and one day to be me again.

I'd been on my own for about a year and a half when I decided I wanted to date. I knew about online dating; that's how Kara and I had met. But things were a bit different now. For one thing, I had a child. And from what I read, single parents tended to feel they had more luck when they could "come out" as parents, in order to frighten away anybody who wasn't ready to deal with that. After I announced that, it became easier to declare my marital status.

I think the Universe knew I needed some help. I tagged a number of individuals as "favourites" to see what would happen. Standing in line at the grocery store with Ben, I looked up and one of those individuals was standing in front of me. Even though I saw only her profile, her faux-hawk and thick black glasses were unmistakable. She was shopping in my neighbourhood because the grocery store across from her apartment had just closed, which was way beyond a coincidence. Amy messaged me that evening.

I smiled and sighed, reading her timid, almost fearful, yet verging on elated question, "What do you mean you work intuitively?" I know this tone. It usually goes with a look I'm deeply familiar with. The look I get when people learn something about me that makes them uncomfortable, while also feeling an unexplainable urge to ask more questions.

Amy's effort to remain open instead of being fearful was evident. I knew I had to come clean. Not just that I worked intuitively, but that I worked with anything I needed to, including the departed. When I do Reiki, information is just information, whether it's sounds, words, scents, images, or entities…

Whatever needs to be shared with me by the Universe, that I can understand, comes.

After putting out there that I was a single parent and a widow, it felt impossible to follow up with, "Oh and by the way, I'm also a medium and I talk to my wife on a regular basis." Yet I went there and

Amy stayed. And what was more, I stayed. I stayed through my intense urge to run when this new relationship opened the depths of my grief. She showed me how much I needed human contact. I stayed even though I tortured myself in and out of permission to be happy. Even when I berated myself and wallowed in the pool of guilt. She stood on the side and patiently waited to offer me a hand up, and I took it even when I wasn't sure I could trust it. And then it occurred to me: *It's not Amy I need to trust, it's me.*

That was when I really started to trust her.

And all the while, my wife still lingered over me like an iron suit of armour. She had kept me safe from everyone but me. The armour stood me up, but as soon as the protective coating fell away, I fell with it. All that fear I had experienced, wondering how I was going to love a stranger and how a stranger could accept my pain — I found myself understanding that I didn't need validation of my pain; I needed validation of my strength.

One night. wrapped in each other's arms, Amy looked at me bemused, and said, "Phoenix." I burst into tears and a wash of disbelief crashed over me. Knowing it must be significant, she pushed me for more information, not even knowing why she said it. I did. It was intuitive.

And I was overcome with the feeling of dread, like the moment you surrender to the air and bungee jump off a cliff. I knew there were things that I was about to give up; my life with Kara, my love for Kara as my only partner, and all my reservations, resistance, and hesitation. That was the night I wrote about the slow incineration of loss, the quiet burn of grief, and the terror of Kara's final moments. I could feel the small flame it lit underneath my heart, as it whispered, "You're going to survive, but you're going to have to burn to do it."

In that moment, I knew survival was possible. That transformation was necessary and in fact had been what God was preparing me for all along. I knew I was going to have to sacrifice my outlived comforts and needs. It was time to burn and become something new. But only if I was brave enough to give up all the things that were not authentically me. To be consumed, if only to stand eye to eye with whatever was on the other side of that fire. I could choose to metaphorically perish and follow the light back to the life that was meant for me.

MEMOS FROM THE UNIVERSE

When my wife passed, the Ginger Menace was only nineteen months, and at that age the ways for him to respond to an event like that were limited. Of course, there was confusion and crying, but he didn't have the words to understand death in a literal way. All he understood, felt, or observed was *change*, which we call loss. All change comes with an inherent feeling of loss; even if it's a positive change, you're required to let go of one thing and accept something else. In the case of my son, he had to, with limited explanation, accept that someone he loved was not there in the same way anymore, and grieve that loss.

After losing his mama, the Ginger Menace regressed on established eating and sleeping habits, and I would learn later, language. As for regression on sleep habits, I regressed a bit as well.

Our bedtime routine had only recently established an uneasy peace, and I was in no way ready to go forward with letting him cry it out. The separation anxiety was too much for either of us, and for a while I let him watch a cartoon on my iPhone in my bed until he passed out. I knew I was not ready to face deciding how to break any comforting habits. Eventually, we transitioned back to the crib, but it was a struggle. The language difficulties, however, were the most challenging of all. I learned that the best way I could help him was by making decisions and being as consistent as possible. This was a challenge sometimes when Mommy had trouble getting off the couch and motivating herself.

As a result, I became a fan of snap decisions. For example, when the Menace was running around the inside of his crib, screaming at the top of his lungs, and I couldn't take it anymore, I decided I was going to let him tire himself out, going in and out to check on him until he learned to *accept* this as the new norm. When he was clamouring for movies all day long as his coping tool turned into a habit, I suddenly made an "only in the afternoon" deal, nudging him toward music as an alternative. When he was demanding bottle after bottle with me, while in daycare all he would use was a big-boy cup, the Universe hit me upside the head to get my attention and asked, "So who's the parent here?"

I'd been wondering for a while when and how we were going to pitch the "bubbas." My boy really loved his bottles. On the one hand, it made my heart ache to think of taking something away from him that was soothing, yet on the other hand, I suspected he was *playing me like a bloody violin*. One day, when my son was around three and a half and still demanding his bottle, I plunked a handful of nipples in a pot of water and set it to boil, then got on with my other tasks.

That's when the Universe took a second swing. A friend phoned. I'd been wanting to speak to Naomi for a couple of days, and soon we were laughing as usual. After a while, I wandered into the kitchen to get away from the loud word-practising the Menace was doing, which was really just a whole lot of noise. Then I inhaled for a moment and thought, *What's that smell?*

It was my new shiny pot, slightly blackened at the bottom and smoking.

Crap, crap, crap! I tore over to the stove and lifted the lid. Where there had been water, there was now a sizzling puddle and seven dingy, cruddy, partially melted rubber nipples puffing a noxious burning stench into my face. I slammed the lid back down and turned off the burner, coughing and closing my eyes at the acrid stench. Naomi asked me what the heck was going on.

"Well," I answered. "I forgot I was boiling nipples. I was thinking about getting rid of them today, but I hadn't totally decided. I guess they're gone now."

Above my head, tumbles of smoke drifted in the beams of light coming from the ceiling. I listened to Naomi laugh as I turned on the fan, opened the back door, took the pot outside, and dumped it in a snowbank. As the putrid smell of burning rubber filled the kitchen and the smoke began to curl toward the living space, I ran to the front door and opened it as well, greeting the postman in my pyjamas, hoping he wouldn't get a whiff of my domestic disaster.

Memo from the Universe received. It said, "He is playing the comfort game with you; Dance for me, my puppet." I knew he would be just fine; it was *my* resistance to change that was the issue.

There was a postscript to this memo: "I know it's tough, so I'm going to try and make this easy for you." Earlier, Amy had creatively suggested arranging with a toy store to take the bottles and "trade" for a new toy, and my daycare lady had suggested I convince him to pack them up because another new baby needed them. I guess those ideas were somewhat vaporized!

Journal Entry

Okay, I can do this. Yes, I happen to have two pre-made bottles in the fridge already, but what if they didn't exist? What if the only option for the Menace to transport milk into his little mouth was his shiny blue sippy cup with Mater on it? Hmmm ... could such a reality exist, like the true reality away from The Matrix, under the flashy surface of reality, where a baby can manipulate his mother like an instrument and get a bottle whenever he wants? Yes, it can!

So I did it. Lunch came and went and we had fun slurping spaghetti noodles with a side plate of avocado, transforming his face into a lunchtime canvas painted red and green. He was still hungry, so after I wiped him down as much as I could, I sent him to the couch with a bowl of apple slices and crackers. I steeled my courage and grabbed the pot off the stove.

"I have to show you something," I said in the most overly sheepish tone I could manage. I sat next to him on the couch. "Mommy made a total bonehead move." I smiled and held out the pot. He peered in, one finger resting on his gappy front teeth and grinned. "Mommy burned the nipples. They're all gone." He knew the phrase "all gone." It was his favourite, as "gone" was one of his first words, coupled with open-hand gesturing.

"So there are no more nipples for bubbas." He reached into the pot. "No!" I squealed. "You don't want those. They're dirty and they stink!" He peered closer, wrinkled his nose, and laughed at me. That was a good sign, when I could play it like I was the butt of a joke. Sigh. Self-deprecating humour can be a handy prerequisite for parenthood. So I pushed my luck. "Would it be all right if we drank milk out of your Mater cup at nap time?"

He nodded. I smiled, returned with the pot to the kitchen, and did a quiet little dance.

I was disproportionally thrilled when I sloshed some milk into his cup and grabbed a soother. Not willing to try giving up both in one day, I presented him with the cup and told him it was naptime. He looked at the cup and frowned his little pouty lip. Before he could start to whine, I turned and went quickly back to the kitchen and said over my shoulder, "Remember, the nipples are gone! We have to use this cup, okay?" Why did this make me feel Machiavellian? I don't know, but I loved it! Sippy cup drunk. *Horton Hatches the Egg* read. The Ginger Menace tucked in. Nap had. Memo received. Thank you.

HALF BAKED

It was January 17, 2014, my father's birthday, and we were visiting my mom. My grandmother's coveted recipe for Orange Chiffon Cake, dad's favourite, was a bone of contention between my mother and grandmother for years — Grandmom did not want to relinquish it. I always pictured them tugging on either end of a recipe card, Mom struggling to hang on to it, Grandmother wrestling it back, and me somewhere in the middle, like a judge watching a white flag tied to a rope in a tug of war. I've enjoyed heckling from the sidelines in similar family scrimmages, occasionally tossing my hat in the ring and tagging one of them out. But in the case of my father's favourite cake, I was always hesitant to enter the fray — until I found myself at my mother's house, and I had a misguided attack of nostalgia. Stupid me.

Anyway, the description of this baked-good battle implies that Grandmom never passed the recipe on, which is not the case. She gave it to my mother all right, but the passing of the torch was more akin to Grandmom handing over a live grenade. It often blew up in Mom's face.

As the Ginger Menace was weaving around our ankles, I said to Mom, "How did you do this with the two of us in the house?"

She looked at me in disbelief. "I didn't! I made it while you were at school. And I usually had to make it several times because the fucking thing never worked."

Perhaps it was safer that we had been away from the expletives? In any case, with the number of notches on my Kitchen Goddess apron quickly multiplying, I felt confident, or even cocky that I could give it the ol' Wilk try.

We started with the recipe, which is officially called: The Betty Crocker Sunburst "Chiffon" Cake. Typed out on a creased paper, yellowed with age, this set of seemly antiquated instructions has seen many kitchen battles. We began with the separating of seven eggs. Now, whenever my mother expressed frustration with this recipe, my grandmother would always ask, "Gayle, did you use brown eggs?"

"Yes, Herta," she would answer.

"Were they freshly laid?" she continued.

"Yes, Herta."

"From the farm?"

"YES, HERTA." She gritted her teeth and answered in the affirmative even if they weren't. I don't really blame Mom, as this cake was always a touchy subject. I'm sure Grandmom did go to a farm for the eggs, but the fervent importance she tried to attach to the gathering of the eggs made me picture her with her hand in an oven mitt shoved under a chicken, waiting for the eggs to pop out, and then booking it home, burning rubber all the way to get it to the Mixmaster in time.

I cracked the first brown store-bought, fridge-cooled egg, cradled the yoke in my fingers, and let the white fall into the bowl. I looked up to see my mother watching me, mystified.

"That's an interesting way to do it," she said.

"That's the way Kara did it." Thinking back to my childhood, however, I remembered a small gadget, which was basically a plastic measuring spoon with holes in it. It was an egg separator, and most likely one of the guess-what-it-is gadgets Mom found in her stocking one year. I assumed that now it was all she ever used. I had gotten so used to the way my wife did things in the kitchen that it felt like the way I had been doing things all along.

So I continued cracking. When I finished, I poured the egg whites lovingly into the seventies'-edition seafoam-green Mixmaster, expounding on the sentimental emotions it evoked after all those years of mixing. I shook in the cream of tartar and, I must admit, I felt quietly arrogant as I watched the egg whites firm up. They looked almost meringue-like, until suddenly their progression to peaks arrested and went backwards. Perhaps it was the dash of ego that threw it off? Well, whatever it was, the white mixture was getting thinner and thinner, and at my feet, the Ginger Menace was losing his mind about something. That's when I felt the urge to swear.

It was easy to see how this dessert nearly drove my mother to want to kill someone. We looked at each other and silently determined that the Mixmaster had its day and should now be kicked to the curb. It must be to blame. It was also obvious that this batch of whites was going nowhere but into an omelette, so I started cracking again. I hoped the cake gods would be kind, even though I had only six brown eggs left (and two white eggs — dare I use them?).

Taking deep breaths, Mom and I took turns whipping the egg whites by hand until they submitted and yielded a light, whipped foam that we were satisfied with. We then began grating the oranges, and after my pathetic attempt, Mom launched herself at the oranges with a vengeance. She produced far more rind from the very oranges I thought were exhausted. It was a bad day to be an orange.

Dumping the rind into the yolk batter, we again stirred by hand, and yet again we had a problem with the consistency — this time at the other end of the spectrum. Now we were giving ourselves hernias trying to stir the batter, which was more like orange cement. Given that the next instruction was to pour the batter slowly and delicately, "drop by drop," into the foamy white bliss, we knew something was wrong. It would be like airlifting a construction crew into a performance of Swan Lake.

We brainstormed. We discussed. And finally we came up with … orange juice. Lots and lots of orange juice. enough to get it to "drip" into the foam. We poured it into the pan, slid it into the oven, and prayed.

We had a glass of wine and then another. When the time came to test the cake, we were feeling hopeful. Our first glance into the oven told us something wasn't right. The cake was half the height it should have been, like a thick pancake. Still, I was optimistic. I pressed it, waiting for a spring back, but got a shrug instead. Undaunted, I placed the pan upside down on glasses to let the cake slowly drop out, but nothing happened. So we turned the pan over and slid a knife around the edge. The outside spring form fell away, yet the bottom of the cake was still firmly connected to the insert of the pan.

This cake was supposed to be so fluffy it would make the angels cry. I could hear weeping all right, just not in the right way. We hacked at it until it came away from the bottom of the pan in chunks. Keeling over with laughter, we chewed and swore. Since I couldn't remember how Orange Chiffon Cake was supposed to taste, I thought it wasn't bad at all. But Mom was incapable of speech as she shook her head snorting. So the Menace and I enjoyed eating the cake over the next few days with tall glasses of orange juice, but Mom refused to touch it.

Now I fear this recipe may be lost to history. My grandmother gleefully celebrated her hundredth birthday. I guess there's nothing to do but make my own mark with a less complicated recipe. Or I can live to at least a hundred and one, and attempt to make this cake for the next thirty-five years of my life and become as stubborn and feisty as Grandmom was. Then when it all goes to hell in a mixer, I'll quietly go to the store and purchase something light and fluffy, from a box. How very Betty Crocker!

FUNNY VALENTINE

"Happy Anniversary, Captain Grief!"

"Happy Valentine's Day, Kelly!"

We clicked mugs of tea at the Second Cup after bundling in from the cold February day. Captain Grief had officially been writing our blog for a year, and it was our blog-aversary.

"My, this is a pleasant exchange…" I shook my head.

"Do you want me to be surly? I can do that…"

"No, no, it just caught me by surprise."

I knew something was up, but for the first time I didn't have a clue what it could be. The Captain looked a little dazed, and if it were possible, gleeful. It was enough to cause me to ask, "Do you have a date or something?"

"Nah. The girl in the super-mailroom is cute, but I think she's straight."

"So what's the deal? You seem kind of mellow and chilled out and…"

At that point, the Captain looked at me with moony eyes and I could see — were those tears? I looked at her in disbelief as she stared back at me and quietly crooned, "Kelly, I love you."

I was speechless for about a minute and a half. "Uh … thanks. What, uh, brought this on?" I leaned in, trying to get a better look at her pupils. They seemed normal, albeit a little watery.

"Oh," she said. "You know, I was just reminiscing, thinking of last year on this day, when I was so griefed-out I couldn't even get out of bed!"

"Yeah, you're right. We're both doing much better than when we wrote my *Valentine's Day Sucks* blog. Wow, that seems like a long time ago, and I was so grumpy. At least now we're less bitter and a *little* less sarcastic."

"Hey, sarcasm is fun, whether or not you're grieving."

"True. I'll treasure the 'Sorry About Your Spouse' card forever," I said. "Add it to my collection."

"Well, you know, I've collected a lot of greeting cards for people surviving Valentine's Day."

"Do share."

Captain Grief reached down the front of her unitard, pulled out a small stack of greeting cards, and spread them on the table so we could look at them. The one on the top caught my eye right away. It had a robber on it holding up Cupid saying, "Drop the candy and leave before I hurt you."

Captain Grief picked one up and handed it to me.

"They're custom made. This is my favourite."

"I can tell." I nodded. The text read, "You have no idea how much of a pain in my ass you are, but I got you a card anyways."

I looked at her and waited for a glint of acknowledgement in the form of smugness, but incredibly enough, she seemed *genuinely neutral about it.*

"So was that it for you? Just a little tender nostalgia?" I asked.

"Well, yes and no. I was thinking about the past year we spent together, even if you have been writing solo without me, jerk." She eyeballed me with a little familiar steel, and then reverted to her sappy expression. "The ups and downs, the laughing, the screaming, the people we cussed out, the lists we made, the demolition, the cakes."

"We did make some good ones."

"Except for the orange anvil that earned you shame and mockery." I glared at her and pointedly looked away. "But it wasn't only that." Her tone took on a slightly serious note. "Writing with you again, on Valentine's Day, and thinking about how far I've come ... I hardly ever destroy stuff anymore. And my tissue bill has gone way down. I'm eating better, sleeping better, and still giving myself permission to do the chucking and snotting if I need to. You helped me so much!" She looked at me with one long, affectionate glance and said, "Kelly, you're my Valentine!"

I was speechless for another a minute and a half, trapped between laugher and heart-thumping awe. Then she handed me a card with my other favourite superhero on it.

"Oh, Captain Grief, that's so sweet! I love Wonder Woman. She was my favourite superhero — until you came along…" And then I felt bad for all the times I called her a bitch, even if she would have agreed with me. "I feel like we should go out to dinner or something to celebrate making it through the year…" *Without killing each other,* I thought.

"Champagne and a four-course meal!" she announced to the coffee shop.

"How about sushi?" I suggested.

"Can we drink sake?"

"Sure."

"Can I play footsie with you under the table?"

"No. Well ... maybe."

"Will you cuddle with me in the cab?"

"Okay, you're getting creepy now."

"Fine, but we're watching *Hancock* when we get home. Charlize Theron is the shit."

"Yes, but you do know she's not a real superhero, right?" I almost clapped my hand over my mouth, and I wondered if the nostalgia would come to an end with me getting slapped.

Instead, she just smiled knowingly and said, "Oh, isn't she?"

"Not unless you know something that I don't." I'll admit that my heart did a little flutter thinking of Charlize in the I'm-going-to-kick-your-ass attire.

"I might."

"Wow." I took a moment to process that with a side of skepticism, and then hope.

"Well, come on, Kel, look at her. How could she *not* have superpowers?"

"True. What about Anne Hathaway as Cat Woman in *The Dark Knight Rises*? Have you met her? Oh, I love you, Anne Hathaway!"

"Don't make me slap you."

"Could you send her a Valentine for me?

Captain Grief looked offended and flashed a card in my face that read, "I hate you." Fair enough.

"Okay, back on task, we're celebrating getting through the hardest year of being a widow. We do the treats and the wine, the movie. We're reconnecting, so what do we do next?"

"Well you know how some couples get to a point in their relationship where things need to be renewed?"

"Sorry?"

"Well, I think that would be a healthy thing to do." She nodded as if she were suddenly on the life-coach spectrum.

"Renew our ... vow?"

"Yeah."

"Hmmm, well I haven't felt the same intense need to write as when we first started. Back then I really relied on finding humour in the everyday muck of grief, but that's changed. These days I find less things I need to transform from frightening to funny. I guess it would be better if we focused on the funny part of *The High-Flying Adventures of Captain Grief*, for the pure joy of it. Even if we don't write every week, it'll still be nice to have this as an outlet."

"So we're going to stick around?"

"Yeah, I think so."

"Okay then, come fly with me ... my funny valentine." She started to serenade me.

"Really?"

She violently mimed a thumping heart on her chest and continued her song, stepping up on the coffee table.

"Captain, no!! Surly, I want surly!"

But she was not deterred. She spread her arms and sang out from her diaphragm to the stunned patrons, "Your looks are questionable, your food undigestable."

"Those aren't the words, Cap."

"... your figure is less than chic, your biceps so damn weak."

"Screw you."

"But you're my faaaaaaaavourite dear old fart," she continued in a loud, shrill voice. I put on my sunglasses and headed to the door. As it closed behind me, I could still hear her painfully pantomiming swoons. "Stay creepy Valentine stay..." She should have left "Funny Valentine" to Michelle Pfeiffer (another sexy Catwoman) and stuck to rude greeting cards.

Journal Entry

You would think I would get that it's hard to let go.

"DENIAL!" as my wife liked to say. "It's not just a river in Egypt." It's one of the verifiable stages of grief. It's also what I've been experiencing for the last few months, when I've thought about ending my stint as Captain Grief.

I've been feeling very guilty about moving away from the Captain. I'm really quite fond of her, and grateful she flew into my life. She was like a dirty, rude, antagonistic angel. Captain Grief has provided so much enjoyment and opportunity for creativity and expression, which really helped increase my confidence. She provided so much laughter and solace for so many people this past year, and she gave me a structure to build a ton of hope for the future.

She was like the most awesome cane — not only did she prop me up, but I could use her to hit things when I wanted to.

I've also started to wonder if other people will miss her, and honestly, if people will still be interested in my writing when she's gone. Then I got an e-card from the Captain herself. On it there was a picture of a woman on a computer. On the screen it said, "So, you created a superhero alter-ego, and now you're using her as a crutch? JUST GIVE IT UP AND EAT SOME CAKE!!"

Yes. It's good to know I can always count on her to be sweet like that! I've leaned on Captain Grief for a long time, but now that I'm out of the cast, she's become more of a shield than a sword. I used to need her, and now I want her because I'm afraid to let her go. For obvious reasons, I've become very attached to her, and I don't want to lose her and all the wonderful things she brought into my life.

I'm pretty positive it's my destiny in life to survive many forms of loss, so I can find my way back to joy. I've written about the considerable list of ways I have experienced loss. I thought of including that here. But after some reflection, I realize that I felt yucky when I read that list over. Things like the loss of a loved one or having a physical disability have a way of defining you in negative terms. My challenge is not to let that happen.

Loss is painful, horrid, and exhausting, but even more so when it's held very close. I think this is why, when the time comes to let go of it, it's so freeing.

There are a number of ways to let go of loss, and artistic expression is a great one. But I'm also entertaining the notion of trying to accept the positive things that have come from the loss I experienced. My book, for example. I wouldn't have been brave enough to write it if I hadn't had the need to be bigger than my fear.

I wouldn't have learned so much about self-care and self-advocacy if I hadn't had to deal with fibromyalgia and other chronic conditions. And the lessons I've learned about pain, grief, and illness have put me in the position to be a compassionate and exceptional healer. In all these positive ways, loss has made me who I am, and any way I look at it, I cannot and would not take that back. And I know that Kara and my father don't want me to either.

Novelist Paulo Coelho said, "If you are brave enough to say goodbye, life will reward you with a new hello." I'm going to wax new-age poetic and say, *I am finding my way into a faith that life won't lead me wrong.* I'm considering some fundamental spiritual concepts. The most important being, Do we really lose what we lose, or is it just that we have to say goodbye to it for a while?

It doesn't mean the loss hurts less, it's just that I am developing more peace with the fact that the loss is there to begin with. And I'm more readily leaving a door open for healing. So it's getting easier to say goodbye. But you know I've never been opposed to a little something sweet to ease the pain of LOSS.

I remember one of the first times I wrote after Kara died; it was also the first time I walked down the street as a widow. The November day was brisk but sunny. A perpetual, surreal haze sat heavy on me, but I suddenly felt like I could breathe, that I was going to be okay. Maybe it was getting away from the house and the gathering of people in it. Maybe it was taking a break from Mommy duty. Or maybe it was just the sun.

I revelled in my aloneness, my anonymousness, and I wandered store to store until I had a strong impulse to buy a new journal. On a day of newness, it was a relief to see a freshly lined page under my hand, and the first thing that inked that page was memoir. Memoir has always been my outlet for the heavy emotions of life and a place to be as existential with my writing as I needed to be.

Captain Grief, on the other hand, was a place to make-believe, a place to play, a place to escape the loss and to learn to confront it in a safe space. Writing my book was like a fresh page, over and over, every week, but memoir is where I live. My creativity is my gift, my power to express my freedom. Captain Grief was my ruby slippers, or rose-coloured slippers in my case. Or silver in the original.

"The Silver Shoes," said the Good Witch, "have wonderful powers. And one of the most curious things about them is that they can carry you to any place in the world in three steps, and each step will be made in the wink of an eye. All you have to do is to knock the heels together three times and command the shoes to carry you wherever you wish to go." Indeed, but Captain Grief is the part of me that always remembers that.

When I first began with Captain Grief, and my friends and family started to get to know her, they would often refer to her in moments when I was attempting to be brave.

"Put on the cape!" they would say.

And I would. I learned to slip into that unapologetic alter ego when I needed to take care of myself or my son. I donned that persona when insecurities or the Major Evils came tromping through my life. I took a breath, put on the cape, and I gave those villains something to think about!

Then, slowly, and without noticing it was happening, I felt stronger, happier, and more inclined to laugh at my misfortunes than ever before. There were days when I truly felt I could soar with the eagles because I had something better than feathered wings! I had a slinky skin-tight suit and an endless sky where I was the only one who got to make the rules, and I didn't care who was watching.

This attitude infiltrated my life, and the singing, dancing, cooking, writing, laughing me has emerged.

When I look back at the soundtrack of my life, I hear ample bawl-your-face-off music, but things are slowly starting to change. First, those songs don't make me cry as much. Sure, if they catch me off guard in a mall … But the other thing is, the female power ballads are really coming in handy!

Looking up favourite artists on 8Tracks, I found a mix titled, "I Can and I Will." As the Pink-heavy mix cycled through, I heard "Brave" by Sara Bareilles for the first time, and before I knew it I was singing about being brave at the top of my lungs. "Stronger" by Kelly Clarkson was making a regular appearance, and who wouldn't feel like a superhero with the lyrics from "Roar" by Katy Perry? The best "I am woman" video (and the best tiger) I've ever seen!

I was also introduced to a new artist I hadn't heard before. To all who know me, I have long had a bitter dislike for country music, but it seems to sidle its way into my life sometimes, and I discover songs that I like. "Follow Your Arrow" by Kacey Musgraves has pierced my heart and my funny bone. It's a super silly, super sexy song that I killed myself laughing at when I looked up the video. This artist definitely has a sense of humour. Her costume was like Daisy Duke meets Country Barbie in Wonder Woman's pants! (Wow, that sounded way more dykey than I thought it would ... go me.) It was love at first listen.

Now that these new, well-loved tracks are running in my head, I know I'm changing. I think it's time for me to fly on my own. And now that Captain Grief has launched me from her bow, it's time to leave her behind.

Captain Grief allowed me to incorporate *her* character traits into *my* persona, while leaving ample room for tears, anger, and snot. Despite her own anguish, she has unarguably allowed me to experience laughter, confidence, and joy. On a picnic on Toronto Island, my friend Faith asked me, "Did you invite Captain Grief?"

"Nah," I answered. "She's a bitch."

Well, as it turns out, the lines between us are starting to blur, and in a few areas, they've all but disappeared. The queer superhero in my head and in my heart is merging with me. At first she was like a brace, so I could stand up straight and remember who I was. Now I'm nervous to take off the brace and go out to find new ways and spaces to keep expressing myself, without the flashy costume.

What I had to remind myself of is that Captain Grief, as wonderful a character as she is, is *fictional*. She was a way to bring new and previously untested parts of me to the surface, and I now need to reclaim them as exclusively mine. Captain Grief and her high-flying adventures, however dear to me they are, have outlived their usefulness, and I need to let them go. But before I do, I'd like to share something special with you. Let's call it a parting gift, which is also a present to myself.

As befitting this wonderful character and the role she played in my life and the lives of others, it's time for her to go out with a Batman-worthy Bam! Biff! Sock! Wham!

Introducing ... the new, improved, less griefy, less angry, less teary, less depressed, less snotty, much happier Captain Grief, drawn by my wonderfully talented girlfriend, Amy Beth.

A.B. Warriner

Captain Grief will always be Captain Grief, and Kelly will always be Kelly. But our first year being widows changed both of us in a million ways (much more than just becoming widows). We found ourselves at our weakest, our strongest, our most sorrowful and most joyous, our most defeated and our most confident. Meaning that we are whatever we want to be and we grieve ... however the fuck we want.

EPILOGUE

I guess I shouldn't be surprised that Captain Grief is just as volatile and overreaction-prone as ever. I sent her a copy of *PinkPlayMags*, with my feature article in it, "Laughing in the Face of Death." It was a tribute, and I thought she would fly over the moon when she received it. *Wrong.*

She was offended and proceeded directly to "overreaction zone" and lashed out at me. I would retaliate if I didn't know exactly how it feels to be overreactive when grieving. Grief has some sharp teeth. It never totally dulls over time. That's why I needed a superhero by my side to fight it. Mind you, "What a Wonderful World" is still one of my favourite songs, and these days I don't mind so much when it comes on the radio. It's how I know Dad is around. Now I can even sing it to the Ginger Menace at bedtime. It's like Dad is reminding me that, even though he's not here to experience it with me, I am here. And I can still allow myself to be awed by the beauty in this world.

But sometimes, when grief clobbers me from behind at exactly the wrong moment, it chews me up and spits me out. So I wasn't totally alarmed when I got the note from Captain Grief, delivered by the Instantaneous Superhero Post System (ISPS). The delivery-hero handed it over, along with a suspicious-looking package that sloshed. I've learned to expect the unexpected from my alter ego, and I see that a tropical vacation did nothing to mellow her out.

Dear Kelly,

Cuba. Is. Fine.

So. I got the copy of the article you wrote about us. I also noticed that you have landed me *not* in the Heroic Epic Super Battle Issue I had hoped for, but instead in the Geek Issue: Nerd Takes Flight. After a year and a half of working together, my partner in crime just sold me out!

What the hell, dude?! I am a legend and it feels like you filed me under Dungeons and Dragons. Would it have killed you to stroke my ego a bit? Do you take all the credit for us too, you limelight-hogging freelancer. I have half a mind to chuck my mojito and fly back to smack you upside the head. Except for the fact that this lawn chair is so damned comfortable, and I have a salsa lesson at two, so think yourself lucky that I am merely going to chew you out! Unless I FedEx you a piranha, then the sentiment will be literal.

Betrayal is such a nauseating emotion. [I could almost hear her sniffling and blowing her nose on a hotel towel.] I thought we had some real nice moments at the end there, but you have thrown me under the media bus! I feel like I just lost my best friend, if you were my best friend, which you weren't, especially now. I thought I was getting better, you know.

I was enjoying myself. I went snorkelling and had a blast chasing the sharks, I had a massage yesterday by the ocean, I knocked back a few piña coladas. I even picked up another vacationing superhero! Madam Mayhem is awesome, but now I can't even remember why. And you know about this because you deal with the same problems!

You know how you're just going along, tickety-boo, feeling groovy, and then something trips you up and lays you flat on your face on the floor of life? *Remember?* You set me up, you creep! Now I guess I'll just have to sit here and ... read the article.

Oh. Well shit, that was sweet. But in the future — and you can travel there by your own damn self — I demand at least an interview and a full-page colour layout of me in a conquering and/or compromising position. I have a great tan and I've really gotten into shape, running tourists hooked onto parasails back and forth across the beach at our club! Madam Mayhem started SVAP there (the Superhero Vacationers Assistance Program). She and I are flying to Havana to do a Cuban Rum History Tour. Don't worry, we're taking the bus back.

Good to know you're all well, and for what it's worth, I do wish you were here sometimes. I loved our conversations, you weirdo. I'm still looking for a "My superhero alter ego went to Cuba, and all she got me is this fucking t-shirt" t-shirt, but I haven't found one yet.

Kiss the kid for me. I'm glad he's getting into trouble once in a while. I loved your update where you played Captain Hook. Though I'm not sure why he wanted to chop your hand off and pretend you had regrown it several times. Talk about habitual loss. I did love when he fed you to the alligator, poked holes in you, and froze your head. What a great kid. I guess I'm proud that I rubbed off on him a bit. Even though last time I came for dinner he sent me to the bathroom for saying a dirty word, the little shit (just kidding!).

I'm really liking the rug rat more and more, you know; he's a resilient little guy. You did a good job helping him cope with some horrible stuff, and he's going to be okay. You both are. You're both too stubborn not to take a rough deal by the nads and chuck it. Oh, and congratulate him for locking you out of the house in your pyjamas. That shit's priceless.

Take care,

Your pal, Captain Grief

xxoo

P.S. Enjoy the rum. You just have to fish out the piranha.

AUTHOR'S NOTE

It's interesting how we have to separate things to understand them. Just as I imagine that repairing a car engine goes much better when you take it apart. I think that's what the Universe was doing when it put Captain Grief in my head. When Kara died I couldn't locate my strength, and looking in the mirror did no good. I had to see it in someone else and ironically that someone was wearing a mask.

Maybe it made it easier to channel myself through an incognito figure in order to be all the things I thought I wasn't. Turns out I am. I'm funny and strong, resilient and gutsy, also hella sarcastic. It's easier to be objective with someone else, so in essence I was just making it easier on myself, to prove I could be my own hero.

I know she is fictional, but for that first year she was a new best friend. Since transitioning my blog from *The High-Flying Adventures of Captain Grief* to the low-flying adventures of *The Ginger Menace*, we've remained joined at the hip and at the heart. Captain Grief is a permanent part of my imaginative world. However, I'm always surprised at how quickly I have access to her. She's in my brain, waiting to leap out and smack me when I need to hear my own voice.

When my dear friend Jennifer Neales, whom I met at the University of Guelph in the Theatre Program, asked me to be in her production #HERstoryCounts, I said an enthusiastic yes! After my speaking role in the annual Singing Out concert, the love of theatre was beginning to boil in my blood again. I had no idea that my alter ego would be making an appearance.

#HERstoryCounts was a reaction to the lack of diversity in theatre, particularly in the case of women of colour. My gay self began workshopping with six other women in February 2016, to write our autobiographical monologues for the performance. In the spring I was still pinning down what I wanted to say. In March I woke on the first morning of a retreat, and during silent meditation, there she was, Captain Grief jumping up and down beside my bed screaming at me to write our story, so rude. She obviously still had stuff to say.

When I write her, I have instant joy and freedom. It's my equivalent to leaping over buildings in a single bound or sailing through a city skyscape on a length of sticky string. So the piece I'd been struggling to write for so long popped out of me that day at the speed of light. Once I introduced the rest of the retreat goers to Captain Grief and they spluttered through the mildly offensive monologue, I knew she was in. From the gasps and number of times they clutched themselves in a riot of laughter, I knew she killed the audition.

It was just the same when I was humming and hawing over which of my projects to move forward with, the traditional memoir or the poetry collage book. My first editor, Keidi Keating, listened to me go on about what my life had been like and the things I had done.

"Captain Grief?" she said. "She's part of the story — no she *is* the story!" She was right, and I began to put all my effort into this book.

However, the play required a much different kind of commitment. The cast loved Captain Grief, but Jennifer reminded me of something her mentor Trey Anthony said during our workshop. It was, "Why? Why this story? Why now?" Jen expounded further to ask me, "Why is Captain Grief here? Why do you need her? Why is she important and what kind of needs or desires does she fill?"

I started thinking about those first critical and heart-crunching months. Everyone was dealing with a brutal shock and despair. Many were angry at the world and life and each other because of Kara's death. However, trapped in it all with my son, I didn't feel like I could. I needed a place where I could scream and rave as much as I wanted to. To be in control of my stories, to make the rules and work with a character who I could always count on to be over the top and 100% unapologetic about her grief. She was freedom.

Then Jen said something that permanently upped the ante. She knew my alter ego, but what she wanted was my story. Where did it start?

"I want you back at the hospital," she said.

I think both of us almost threw up, and I didn't even time travel, except I did. When she asked me what the worst thing I had to deal with was, I began in my head to say, "I hate the night." I actually had to close my eyes and breathe when I came into the mental and emotion space where that feeling existed.

She almost jumped off the little stool in her apartment. "What just happened there?"

What happened is that *I found my way in*. That's how I found myself in a bathrobe and yellow socks, on stage, singing to my son and miming putting him to bed. I slipped into my old skin shuddering and hyperventilating. But if I was going to do this, play this character of myself as I was, I had to go there. I had to go back to that hospital where I was standing beside Kara's mother, shouting at Kara to fight as they brought her back flatline after flatline. Then it was over, and life began anew and I told my story.

I picked up my pen that day for the #HERstoryCounts production and just like when Kara passed away, Captain Grief was there when I needed her, saying "Nice of you to show up. Now stop slacking off and write the fucking thing."

Being here without you is unbearable. The sheets still smell like you. I've been here for five months and you are everywhere I look— "Ben! Gentle with the cat!"— *I can't escape, I can't fall apart, I can't grieve. I'm mom. I—* "Get that out that out of your nose!"—*No, I have to keep it together and smile and I can't get mad* [I step on a toy car]— "Motherffffing cars!" [Breathe, breathe. Look at my sweet baby boy.] "C'mere, you rascal! Let's make these cars drive … Hey! You ran me off the road you little stinker." *I can't get mad. I can't.*

That's when I knew I had to put on the cape.

So I flung off the bathrobe, and there she was in the flesh. Triumphant superhero pose, hands on hips, hair flying in the fictitious wind and then crumpling into a pathetic, huffy monologue beginning:

Captain Grief's First Journal Entry (where I become Captain Grief in the play)

Valentine's Day sucks!! Know where I am the first V Day after my spouse died? Bed! [Incredulous noise at obvious answer.] If Hallmark made a card for that, it would read: Welcome to your new and improved Valentine's Day suckfest! Why fight the crowds for a fancy dinner or get trampled on your way to the cab? Well you don't have to, not when your wife has kicked the bucket!! And you know what? I try, I really do. I make a concentrated effort to be okay. Kelly is writing a blog about *me*, Captain Grief, and I can't even get out of bed to take leak. I have to pee in the empty soup bowl on the floor.

Captain Grief didn't set the bar high, she *was* the bar; coaxing me, chastising me, imploring me to get up off my ass and be the powerhouse I was. She is the part of me that wants me to expect more of myself, to be proud and brave and unbroken in this new life that is mine, like it or not. I knew if Captain Grief was going to show up in the play, I owed it to both of us to make her proud.

I needed to have my costume sorted out quickly, so one sunny afternoon on Queen West my son and I crept into a costume shop and I asked the sales lady for a superhero unitard, preferably in blue. While The Ginger Menace was fixated on Harry Potter props, she rummaged through her stock and I stood there nervously. She gave me a few contenders and I sheepishly entered the change room.

I stepped out again for her to zip me in and then looked at my son. His face was literally like the Santa Claus parade when the head honcho makes his festive appearance, like I had leapt out of a phone booth to a heroic trumpet blast. The joy radiating from his little face was thrumming in the atmosphere, not to mention his chortling and utter bliss at seeing his mother in a unitard.

I felt it. Yup; this was the one. I looked in the mirror and thought, *Shit, shit, shit*, then *Why not?*, then, *Well who the fuck cares?* When I put on the gold belt (that magically appeared in a used clothing store we frequented) and the banana-yellow soccer socks (I discovered in the sock shop that just happened to pop up on my route to my writing workshop) and the eye cooling gel mask — I looked at myself again. *Shit*.

I read somewhere that Lynda Carter once told someone when she was wearing her Wonder Woman suit she never once felt degraded or ashamed. I concur. I felt strong and sexy, and no one was going to tell me what to do or not do. The way that slippery, silky fabric coated me from wrist to neck to ankle, it was like I was back in the beloved jazz dance class I took before I was diagnosed with chronic pain when I was twelve.

The way the golden belt shone in the lights, the way people reacted to my body and my audacity to put it all out there with pride and no apology, it made me feel like I was someone who had always been on the inside and now was on the outside. I was a hero and it was delicious. And I didn't give a flying fuck what people would say because it was about my story, my life, my needs, and my resolve.

Captain Grief is a highway to all the characteristics I already possessed. She is a pal, a pain in the ass, and the best antidepressant possible.

And as I sit here with Kara's original Superman and Green Lantern action figures, I know that Kara is more than appreciative of the service she has done her wife. There are still times when I am laid out on rock bottom by grief. But I know if I can find the hero inside of me, I will never be alone again.

POP QUIZ

Did I forget to tell you we would be time travelling to 2016 for a pop quiz? Well, we are and this is it. It was actually written in celebration of the four-year anniversary of Kara's death. Now that I have a number of annual loss-fests under my proverbial belt, I have been slowly changing the way I acknowledge grief. The key to a gentler approach when grieving is *compassion.*

I try to gather myself in and be my own best comfort. I trust myself to take care of my own needs and ask for support. To decide what *I* want. And now, more often than not, it's a table of friends telling stories. It's a literal feast. It's anything that can help me be more relaxed, centred, and expressive in the act of grieving. It's celebrating love and all the wonderful ways it is still in abundance in my life. It is also continuing to give myself permission to laugh and take things way less seriously than they need to be. Hence, the silly party game I whipped up.

TRIVIAL PURSUIT: THE KARA EDITION

1. How many times did Kara jump out of a plane?
    A) Once
    B) Twice
    C) Five times
    D) Twenty times
    E) One hundred times

2. When was the last time Kara willingly wore a dress?
    A) When she was 20
    B) When she was 9
    C) When she was 7

3. Who was Kara's favourite superhero?
    A) Batman
    B) Superman
    C) The Green Lantern
    D) The Hulk

4. What cartoon character did Kara laugh like?
    A) Ernie
    B) Elmo

C) Buzz Lightyear
   D) Cookie Monster

5. What things has Kara carried in the car?
   A) A jack
   B) An emergency blanket
   C) A first aid kit
   D) An engagement ring
   E) a bottle of port
   F) An axe
   G) All of the above

6. Which sports did Kara participate in? (It's not in the book. I just wonder if you can guess.)
   A) Hockey
   B) Football
   C) Rugby
   D) Cheerleading
   E) All of the above

7. What misdeed was she punished for with cheerleading? Okay, so you have to guess for this one too, but how can I not provide this fact. I know — fiendish!)
   A) Toilet papering the coach
   B) Spiking the punch
   C) Streaking at half time
   D) Letting a mascot animal loose in the other team's change room

BONUS ROUND

What is my favourite saying from the Bullshit Button?
   A) Now that was grade A bullshit!
   B) If bullshit were money, you would be a millionaire!
   C) Everybody put on your helmets, bullshit is being flung!
   D) Bullshit alert! Bullshit alert!

Answers:

1. E: One hundred times

2. C: Seven years old (it was the Winnie-the-Pooh dress)

3. B: Superman

4. D: Cookie Monster

5. G: All of the above

6. D: Cheerleading

7. D: Letting the mascot loose in the rivals dressing room. Seriously, you can't make this shit up!

Bonus. C: Everybody put on your helmets, bullshit is being flung!

ABOUT THE AUTHOR

Kelly lives in Toronto with her son, Ben (aka, The Ginger Menace).

She is a freelance writer for *PinkPlayMags,* a quarterly LGBTQ+ publication. She is also a registered reflexologist and Reiki master at the Inner Arts Collective. Kelly loves hearing people's stories and believes in the healing power of giving yourself permission to share them, as you are the only one who can.

Creative writing is not just her craft; it is the way she maintains her health and happiness. Writing has allowed her to record and celebrate memories of the dearest places and people in her life. Being a holistic practitioner has increased her desire to use artistic expression as an instrumental healing tool. For this reason, she has begun to facilitate other people's creative journeys through a creative writing course: Narrative Healing Workshop.

Kelly is a memoirist and poet, as well as a blogger. She began her original blog, *The High-Flying Adventures of Captain Grief*, as an outlet to process the death of her spouse and her induction into the world of single-parenthood. After this, she began to write a queer parenting blog for *PinkPlayMags* called *The Ginger Menace*, now reincarnated to be *The Ginger Gent* (www.pinkplaymags.com). She also writes her own blog, *Brave.Creative.Me.*

Kelly writes fiction as well as nonfiction and short stories. "Going to Market" was published in the anthology *Beer and Butter Tarts*, a Canadian food journal published by Stained Pages Press. She also had two pieces of poetry selected for *The Annual Her Heart Poetry Anthology* in 2018, and she was published in the November 2019 issue of *Maclean's* with the opinion piece, "A Widowed Mother to Her Son: 'Your Small Life Was So Powerful, It Saved Mine.'"

Kelly also appeared (as herself *and* her caped alter ego) in the inaugural performance of #HERstoryCounts, a theatre project devoted to telling the autobiographical stories of women who have been silenced, in particular women of colour. Kelly loves performing her creative pieces, and as a new author, she looks forward to bringing many serious to semi-serious (but mostly hilarious) projects to the world, in the hopes of amusing, inspiring, and comforting as many people as possible.

For more information about Kelly, go to www.kellywilk.ca.

Kelly's note: For current Captain Grief content (yes, the old girl is still kicking and pissed) go to www.captaingrief.com or The High-Flying Adventures of Captain Grief on Facebook to join our laughing, crying community!

BIBLIOGRAPHY

Annis, Leslie. "Lannis: Gallows Humour and an Introduction." *The Mrs*. April 18, 2013.

Bareilles, Sarah and Jack Antonoff. "Brave." *Blessed Unrest*. Epic Records, 2013.

Carey, Mariah. "I Miss You Most at Christmas Time." *Merry Christmas*. Columbia, 1994.

Cars, Cars 2 and *Maters Tall Tales*. Pixar Animation Studio, Walt Disney Pictures, 2006–2018.

City of Angels. Warner Brothers Pictures, 1998.

Collins, Sarah. *Real Simple*. New York: Meredith Corporation, 2000.

Choclat. Miramax Film, 2000.

Coehlo, Paulo. *The Alchemist*. New York: Harper Collins, 1988.

Connie and Carla. Universal Studios, 2004.

Emmons, Sasha. *Todays Parent*. 1984.

Fey, Tina. *Bossy Pants*. New York: Little Brown and Company, 2011.

Firefly Creative Writing. Creative writing coach and retreat facilitator Chris Kay Fraser. March 13, 2018. fireflycreativewriting.com

Musgraves, Kacey. "Follow Your Arrow." *Same Trailer Different Park*. Mercury Nashville, 2013.

Gaye, Marvin. "How Sweet It Is (To Be Loved by You)." Tamala, 1964.

Ghost. Paramount Pictures, 1990.

National Geographic. 1888–2018.

Gore, Lesley. "It's My Party. I'll Cry If I Want To." Mercury Records, 1963.

Hancock. Columbia Pictures, 2008.

"Here in Spirit." *Mike Holmes Makes it Right*, Season 2 Episode 8. HGTV, August 26, 2014.

Imagine Me and You. Fox Searchlight Pictures, 2005.

Jackson, Michael. "Thriller." Epic, 1982

The L Word. MGM Worldwide Television, Showtime, 2004–2009.

The Loomba Foundation. Raj Loomba. June 21, 2013, from www.theloombafoundation.org

Lowery, Sassafras. *Lost Boi*. Vancouver: Arsenal Pulp Press, 2015.

McLachlan, Sarah. "Wintersong." *Wintersong*. Nettwerk/Arista, 2006.

Moore, Clement Clarke. *'Twas The Night Before Christmas*. New York: Sentinel, 1823.

Murray, Anne. "Hi-Lili Hi-Lo." *There's A Hippo in My Bathtub*. EMI Music Canada, 1977.

Monsen, Avery and Jory John. *All My Friends Are Dead*. San Francisco: Chronicle Books, 2010.

Nunsence. Off Broadway Productions Worldwide, 1985

Perry, Katy. "Roar." *Prism*. Capitol Records, 2013.

Silver Linings Playbook. The Weinstein Company, 2012.

"The Time Warp." *The Rocky Horror Picture Show*. By Richard O'Brien and Richard Hartley. Performance by Tim Curry. 20th Century Fox, 1975.

To Wong Foo, Thanks for Everything Julie Newmar. Universal Pictures, 1995.

Pfeiffer, Michelle. "My Funny Valentine." *The Fabulous Baker Boys*. Song By Richard Rogers for Babes in Arms. 20th Century Fox, 1989.

Queer As Folk. Red production Company, 1999.

Victor/Victoria. Hollywood Studios, 1982.

Viorst, Judith. *Alexander and the Terrible, Horrible, No Good, Very Bad Day*. New York: Atheneum Books, 1972.

Water, Sarah. *Tipping the Velvet*. United Kingdom: Virago Press, 1998.

Winterson, Jeanette. *Oranges Are Not the Only Fruit*. United Kingdom: Vintage, 2001.

Wonder Woman. Warner Brothers, 1975.

The Walking Dead. AMC Studios, 2010–2018.

Printed in the USA
CPSIA information can be obtained
at www.ICGtesting.com
JSHW021154240624
65224JS00004BA/24